Sing to the Moon

Tales from the Kitten Cam

Written & Illustrated by

Jill Pickford

D0557447

Great Circle Productions ● Colchester, UK

ISBN: 1544740387
ISBN-13: 978-1544740386

DEDICATION

For John and Chris, and animal rescuers everywhere.

TABLE OF CONTENTS

ACKNOWLEDGEMENTS

More thanks than I can properly express go to Susan Hoyle Bailey, Mar Penner Griswold, and Nancy Freeman for getting this project on the road, for raiding their piggy banks and for giving up their free time to do all the proof reading, editing and layout. They are my "without whom's." Also to Joan Hutchins Friel and Lynne Dixon for jumping in to help with the promotion and marketing of the book and to Nancy again for going the extra mile to be our cheerleader at the AJCS and KCC. Thanks too to Connie Gabelein at Purrfect Pals for her help throughout.

Thanks also go to those Critter Room families who allowed me to raid their photographs for source material for the illustrations.

I would be derelict in my duty, too, if I didn't acknowledge all the rescuers and fosterers whose dedication and compassion inspire this community every day. So, to the team at Purrfect Pals, to Sarah, Shelly, Cassie, Janice, Andrea, Sonja, Margo, Jenia, Paul, Shona, and anyone else who I may have forgotten, goes my undying admiration for actually doing what others just talk about.

And finally, I am grateful to everyone I have met, physically and virtually, through the medium of the kitten cams, whose enthusiasm for these wee tales have made this book possible and whose friendship I value more than I can say.

Oh... and whatsisname, too. You know... big fella... moustache ... glasses... likes donuts...

THANK YOU. Jill xxx

FOREWORD

My first impulse when I was asked to write the foreword to this collection of Jill's wonderful stories was to rework my "Road to Ripley" post from a couple of years ago on Facebook. After all, that has gained many complimentary comments when I posted it, and is strongly concerned with Purrfect Pals' and other shelters' missions. However, besides being incredibly lazy on my part, I decided on reflection that it would not really fit the bill: it is too focused on Ripley and her family, and doesn't focus on fostering and the phenomenon that is The Kitten Cam community. So I looked back over the nearly four years that have elapsed since we adopted Ripley, and how we have seen this phenomenon develop.

I believe I am correct in asserting that it was with Ripley's litter that FDJ's cam went viral (though perhaps that is a slightly infelicitous word when used in conjunction with cat shelters), and for the following two years after that I attended every one of FDJ's litter adoptions. I acted as an unofficial photographer, posting many hundreds of photographs on Facebook, so that those who were unable to attend the events could get at least a feel of them. Participating in the chat channel on Livestream after each event, I began to understand just how widespread the Kitten Cammers were, but I would have been very skeptical if someone had told me that in 2014 people would come from as far away as

Western Australia (Hi, Robyn!) and Europe to spend a few days with people they had never met, and take part in a vacation based around the Average Joe Cat Show. As it was, I was amazed, and continue to be amazed by the dedication of the organizers and attendees of the three Kitten Cam Cons that have taken place in Seattle so far, and the three that will have taken place in Europe by the time this book is in your hands.

From my perspective as a member of the Board of Directors of Purrfect Pals, I am delighted that *Sing to the Moon* adds yet other element that helps us in our mission to end cat homelessness in the Puget Sound region. The first Kitten Cam Con made front page news on the Seattle Times, and Elisa Jaffe broadcast a segment on KOMO4 with attendees, and Ripley herself—the simple fact that so many people had come from so far was a news story in itself, and it gained good local publicity for Purrfect Pals.

From my perspective as a cat fan and an occasional Cammer myself, I also appreciate how much fun it is to be around this wonderful group of people, and how quickly they have solidified into a real supportive and caring community who have helped not just the cats and shelters, but also each other. I know for a fact that many members of the community have formed deep friendships, and received support and encouragement when they have been in difficult and challenging circumstances. My life was irrevocably changed by adopting Ripley and the way it drew me into working with Purrfect Pals, and anyone who attended the 2015 Kitten Cam Con dinner at Ivar's on Lake Union will also know of the way quite a few other lives have been put back together by the Kitten Cam Con community.

And while this is all very good and rewarding, it does leave me with somewhat ambivalent feelings. The mission of Purrfect Pals and other shelters is basically to end cat homelessness, but that would mean no foster litters on cams, no excitement, joy, or sadness at the events being streamed—I've lost count of the number of times people have told me about the cheers and tears when Ripley's red cross became a green tick on 23rd February 2013. While I and many others who are working to end cat homelessness are aware that the success of our mission would mean the end of this phenomenon we are all too aware that this will not be happening in the next few years and we are most appreciative that the community is there to support our mission and share in the journey. As long as there are cats needing homes and cams to broadcast them, let the Kitten Cam community flourish!

James "Mr Ripley" Petts
October 2016

A NOTE FROM THE EDITOR

I discovered Foster Dad John's Kitten Cam slightly after Jill did—at the tail end of Rosemary and the Spice Kittens. Cute kittens, I thought, but then they were gone. I did not fall head over heels in love with the Cam until Ripley came onto the scene with her incredible eyes and her incorrigible and adorable kittens.

Little by little I was drawn into the kitten cam community and then along came my first Adoption Day. I cried real tears that day—tears of sorrow when I feared for Ripley's future, and tears of joy when that lovely English gentleman held our beautiful girl in his arms and promised her a forever home.

Jill's stories mesmerized me from the first. They have never failed to make me laugh or cry—and either way I am grabbing for the tissues to wipe away tears. (This made even the minimal editing required just a tad difficult, let me tell you!)

Local friends sometimes wonder why I support Purrfect Pals in Seattle when I live on the other side of the country. I do support two area cat rescues but I feel that "a rising tide lifts all boats" and this wonderful global community we have built helps not only cats and kittens all over the world but humans as well. This book provides many glimpses into the magical, mysterious, and heart-warming interactions between Felis domesticus and Homo sapiens.

So—sit down, grab a box of tissues and plunge into Jill's world. This book is a treasure for the ages.

Mar Penner Griswold, Buffalo, NY
March 2017

Post Script: You will notice that since the author is British, British words, colloquialisms and spellings have been faithfully maintained for this manuscript—however, as a nod to the Americans in the audience, American punctuation is used throughout (well, with only one exception, but we will leave that for you, dear reader, to discover!).

As you enter the magical world of *Sing to the Moon*, you may come across words that seem strange to you such as "Chickenfish" and "hoomin." If you are new to the Critter Room experience, take a moment to visit the *Sing to the Moon* Facebook page at www.facebook.com/groups/Singtothemoon and download a free glossary/explanation of terms. Feel free to ask questions of the author on the page and she will happily answer.

Then prepare to immerse yourself into a beautiful world of cats—a world full of laughter and not without a few tears.

INTRODUCTION

In the early autumn of 2012, finding myself alone and bored in my office, I clicked on a link which someone had posted on a message board and was instantly transported to a world of magic and wonder. In the clean white surroundings of a large kennel cage was a cardboard box turned on its side, and inside the box was a beautiful calico cat with a magnificent fluffy tail, together with her four tiny kittens.

Rosemary's Spice Kittens were a couple of days old at the time and not very active, so I amused myself by following the chat. Mentions were made of weigh-ins, milk bars, whappy paws and a mysterious being called John (this was before the Foster Dad was added).

For the next couple of weeks, John was only a voice and two disembodied arms, but I watched fascinated as he weighed kittens, cuddled mama, nursed upset tummies, spoke sternly to little Pepper about the need to part with her umbilical stump, and stuck new googly eyes on Chickenfish (Hail!). Once the kittens were big enough, I became acquainted with the rest of the kitten Disneyland that is The Critter Room. The Mewniverse, the Batcave, the Enterprise and the Tardis all became as familiar to me as my own furniture (and, in some cases, better quality) and I became inexorably sucked into the extraordinary human community that was already growing around the kitten cam.

The following summer, Kari and her Mythbusters were in residence and a hot spell prompted John to bring in a portable air conditioner to cool the room. Kari's reaction to the noise it made inspired me to write my first short piece in the form of a letter from Kari to her mother. I posted it on my Facebook page and John shared it on The Critter Room page and the rest, as they say, is history.

Along with my fellow Kitten Cammers, I have watched happily for hours while a man swept a floor; I have watched after a blown light bulb plunged the room into darkness; I have watched while the view was nothing more than the gaping black maw of Fishbed, or the evil red eye of the hideous white rat creature (you probably know the one). I have shared in triumphs and tragedies, laughter and tears and almost overwhelming levels of cute and, occasionally, I have been inspired to write about it.

So here, for your delight and delectation, are most of my stories and poems gathered together in one volume, lavishly but nonetheless incompetently illustrated, by me, with crayons and felt-tips. I apologise if I've coloured outside the lines.

All profits will be donated to Purrfect Pals, without whom none of us would have met.

Jill Pickford, Colchester, UK
March 2017

KARI'S LETTER HOME

It was the summer of 2013 and there was a heat wave in Seattle, so John hired a portable air conditioner to keep Mama Kari and her Mythbuster kittens cool and comfortable. Mama Kari was less than impressed by the noise it made…

Dear Mum,

Sorry it's been so long, but… well… I'm afraid things didn't turn out quite the way I planned. Yes, yes… I know you warned me that they all only wanted one thing, but the ginger guy was so charming, and I'm a self-confessed sucker for an exotic oriental and the gentle tabby brought me the corpse of a rat with the head still on. How many guys would be that generous, huh? Anyway, long story short, suddenly there was no room at the inn and I found myself shoved in a box and delivered—with no ceremony at all—to what I can only assume was some kind of maternity hospital. Didn't even have time to pack my blankie or mousie. I miss mousie. After that, we (it was WE by that time) were dispatched like luggage AGAIN, this time to a big, scary cage thing with a big, scary hoomin. I'll tell you more about the hoomin later.

Anyway… I hope you're not too mad with me, because you'd just adore the kids. Four of them, all cute as buttons. Mum, my backside isn't that big, is it? I know you'd tell me if it was. I only ask because, well, every time I went to sit down inside this cage thing, one of the babies had managed to wriggle its way under my butt. I swear I never saw them move but, lo and behold, without fail it was, "Squeak, squeak!" another squished kitten. So embarrassing! It's a good job nobody was watching.

So—the hoomin—I think it's a he. It's hard to tell without getting a good look at... you know. So I'll say "he" for the sake of argument. He's ENORMOUS, but he has soft hands and a nice, gentle purr. He gives good rubs and scritches and furfles my ears and I trust him with the babies. They like to climb him, although he's a bit slippery and they have to grip on tight. He smells like the streets and good food and cats. I wish he came to see us more often, but I feel we are safe here. There's a smaller one too. He seems to have an obsession with digging up the poop we have just buried and collecting it. They are a strange species.

You'll be glad to know that I waited until the proper time to perform the ritual. I sat in the window and sang to the full Moon and she told me that the kittens' names were Mordoc, Slayer of Voles; Kayleb, He who Dances with Shadows; Elinora, Lighter than the Air, and Shara, With Eyes like the Summer. Much as I like the hoomin, he seems incapable of memorising their names, no matter how many times I correct him. He just grunts strange noises at them. Sometimes, I don't think he's very bright. Elinora lived up to her name the other day and jumped all the way up to the window. I was proud of her. She fell off shortly afterwards, but it was a good first try.

Hey, one thing though. The other day, it was getting real warm and we were all feeling snoozy and lazy when this cacophony started up in the corner of the room. It was making a noise like Uncle Feyodah, He who Poops in Closets used to do when that big tortoiseshell from next-door-but-one came in and stole his kibble. I tried to calm the kittens down by singing to them, but Kayleb is a bit "sensitive", if you know what I mean, and I just seemed to be making matters worse. So now, when the noise starts up, I just sing to myself instead and remember Uncle Feyodah and all the family. I think I might be accidentally summoning a spirit from beyond The Bridge, though, because whenever I sing, the room gets colder. It's very odd.

The kids are growing like weeds now. Elinora and Mordoc look a lot like our side of the family. Shara and Kayleb look more like their dads, but it can't be helped. I love them anyway. It'll soon be time for them to become independent, which will be sad in a way, but I cannot wait for them to step out into the world and fulfil their destinies. I've talked to the girls in the hope that they won't fall into the same trap as I did, but you know girls (of course you do ha ha) they never listen to their mothers. Mordoc is healthy and floofy just like us and—well, sensitive kittens can make their way in the world too, so I'm not worried about Kayleb. He will be a heartbreaker. My girls, too. They're bold and beautiful and will rule their kingdoms with wisdom, grace and only minimal use of claws and teeth.

As for me, I don't know what will become of me. I miss my bed and my mousie and I would love to have a proper home again with a hoomin to worship me and a lap to lie on. It may be that those days are over forever, in which case I must find a new path. I'm beginning to wonder if I might have magical powers, because... and I can't really explain this... I am absolutely certain that I am being watched. I know they are there. I can feel them. I hope they like what they see.

Will write again soon.

Keep safe and warm,

Your loving daughter,

Zathira, With Eyes like the Sun and Moon

RIPLEY'S ADVICE TO KARI

Mama Ripley and her exceptional kittens were long since gone to their forever homes, but the story of Ripley's last-minute adoption by the "Nice English Bloke" just had to be told.

Hello Kari,

I hope you don't mind me calling you Kari, since we're being informal and... well, my mum never performed the ritual so She never named us. It was tough enough for mum to find enough food so we didn't go hungry, and I'm afraid the niceties got overlooked sometimes. She did her best, though, and I'm grateful to her.

I hope you've found my mark. If you haven't, look for it under the window, which was my special place while I was in the big white den. The other girls left their marks too. I found Rosemary's straight away because it was the newest and it was still glowing. It was a big comfort to me. It told me that everything would be OK.

Do you want to hear my story? I think it will help you, so listen up while I tell it. I was born on the wrong side of the tracks, for sure. I don't want to go into details about how it was hard to find enough food or to find a warm place to lie down—all that is in the past and best left there. I spent most of my time out-of-doors, where at least the air was fresh and there was a chance of a mouse or two and... well, you know how it is. The tabby from the parking lot was kind and showed me where the plumpest mice

4

were to be found and... oh! But that big, long-haired drifter was just the most handsome dude I've ever seen. I still dream about him some nights...

Kari... you think four is hard work? Try five! And what's more, they were all born grey! You know what that means—I'd not done right by my babbies while they were cooking. I felt so ashamed. I'm afraid it made me a little short in the temper department and, although I was taken to a lovely place with a soft bed, I'm afraid I disgraced myself. I would like to apologize to that cat in person one day. I hope his fur grew back OK. Anyway, the end result of our... er, close encounter was that I was shipped out to the big white den with the big white cage and the big white hoomin. Yes... that hoomin. I thought it was some kind of tree at first, but then he purred at me and let me boop his hand and he was so gentle with the babbies. They adored him.

Ha ha! I can't help wondering what names She would've given my brood, if I'd done the ritual. "Ash, He who Doubles in Weight Daily"; "Bishop, with a Face like a Pansy"; "Parker, where the Hell has he gone Now?" Ah... what fun they had together, my lovely, lovely kittens.

I understand that feeling of being watched, too. At first, I thought it was the little yellow god with the staring eyes. Has he manifested himself to you, too? He bothered me at first, I don't trust a creature who stares so intently but says nothing, even if he is an immortal. But then he cuddled my little daughter when she was having bad dreams and soothed her to sleep, so I said "hail" to him, which seemed to be what he expected and we lived in peace after that.

I loved my time in the den. It was the best time of my life... up to that point. But, you see, Kari, a day is coming that you should be prepared for. Your time in the den is coming to an end—I know you can sense it. When it was our day to leave, we were taken to a bright, shiny and noisy place with strange hoomins everywhere. We took The Oath together and pledged to uphold The Code then, one by one, my babbies were taken from me and I was left alone. I'd just told my kids to be brave, but it's easier to say than to do and I felt very, very afraid. I don't know how long I was there on my own. I hunkered down in the hope that no-one would see my fear and time seemed to stand still but, suddenly, I felt a rush of warmth, from the tips of my whiskers right through to my toe pads. It was like the sun emerging from behind the clouds and my spirits were lifted. It was as if I could hear a thousand voices all shouting, "Yay!" Then hands reached into the cage and I was lifted out and I gazed up for the first time into the face of a hoomin… MY hoomin! I cried and cried and clung on tight so he wouldn't leave me behind and we cuddled for the longest time, before we left the shiny place forever… together.

You see, Kari, I'm as ordinary as you are exotic, as plain as you are beautiful, yet here I am, with my big sisters, and two hoomins to care for whom I love dearly. There will be love for you too, and snacks and sleeps and cuddles. And don't be afraid for the babbies either, for they will go on to great things. I am so proud of my boys and girls. So young, yet they are teachers, comforters, counsellors, comedians and companions and so, so beautiful, every one of them. And my boy Ash… well, he's just the spitting image of his father. Don't tell him I said so, though.

So, leave your mark for the next lonely mother to find and, when you have moved on, listen for us in the darkest hour of the night, when The Moon has gone to sleep and the world is quiet. You know that murr that's right down low? The one that seems to come in on the breeze, just on the edge of hearing—that you feel through your paws and whiskers? That will be us. We are waiting for you.

And, somewhere out there, they are waiting too.

Good luck,

Ripley

PS: We've all been baffled by the poop thing. Rosemary thinks they probably use it as currency. Rosemary is usually right about these things.

KARI'S CONVERSATION

It fell to Mama Kari—by now renamed Lacey and happily ensconced in her new home—to introduce us to the Great Circle, a means for all our mother cats to keep in touch, using low frequency vocalisation and just a bit of magic.

Mum—it's good to be in touch again...

Well, it has happened just as we knew it would. I am separated from my babies. We will travel separate paths from now on and I must have faith in them to put what they have learned to good use. I know I have prepared them right, but it's hard not to worry just a bit. It's the little things that pop into your head, isn't it? And always when you're about to tuck into your dinner, or drift off to sleep. Who will baff them? Will they bury correctly? Will they clean between their toes? You must have gone through exactly the same thing with us.

As you know, I had no idea where my own road would lead me, but it seems that, after many twists and turns, detours and dead ends, it has led me to the home of these good hoomins. Oh, mum! It's better than I could possibly have imagined! This is such a cosy place, full of soft and warm things (well, apart from the stiff cat, but I'll gloss over that for now) and the hoomins are... well, right. They are cat people. You explained cat people to me a long time ago, but now I understand what you meant. I can tell by the way their hands are relaxed when they touch my head and ears and by the tone of their voices when they purr at me and by the scent of them and their things. These are hoomins who know cats and are known by cats. I have no fears. I know they will keep their side of the pact in full and I will keep mine. We will be happy together. I am not alone here, though. There is another with whom I hope to be friends, but she is missing her sister, lately taken up, so I shall bide my time and be patient with her.

I spent my first day here learning the smells and sounds and sights (that stiff cat is REALLY stiff—I don't understand it at all) and teaching my hoomins where I like to lie down and how I like to be petted and, I'm sorry to say, I didn't give much thought to the babies. But, on the second night, anxious for news, I remembered Ripley's instruction, so I waited until dark and went to the window. The Moon was still up, so I sang a little to Her to give thanks for my good fortune, and then I tucked in my paws and waited until She had disappeared to sleep, not really knowing what to expect. I was just starting to doze off when, suddenly, there it was. First, it was just the tiniest vibration on the end of my whiskers, then it came in through the floor under my paws and spread slowly along my spine and up into my ears. It reminded me of the sound of thunder a long way off, only softer and more musical. I swivelled my ears and stiffened my whiskers to channel the sound into my brain, where it began to resolve itself into something familiar, comforting yet thrilling. The voices of my sisters.

They called me by my proper name and asked me to relate my story and I learned that there are many, many cats who have shared the same experience as me and who remember the white room and the big, kind hoomin and his little companion with the poop fixation. They talk together often and Ripley (man, that girl hears some gossip!) was able to tell me about the kittens and that they are all safe and well and living in the homes of good hoomins. I am excited for them and can sleep easy now, knowing that all is well with them. My new companion joined us for a while. She told us how lonely she had been since her sister had gone, but Rosemary was able to teach her how to look into the night sky to find her sister's eye, which watches over her from within the constellation called The Queen, at the Moon's right hand. She seemed to be comforted by this and I have hope that she will come to accept me as a friend—maybe, one day, even as her sister.

And now I've found you again, mum. We can talk to each other about the old times, good and bad, and things that have happened and things that will happen. We can talk about friends and family, warmth and comfort, security and the goodness of hoomins. We will no longer need to talk about being cold, or hungry, or afraid or lonely.

We are home.

TALL TAILS 1: ASH BOND

The whole world fell in love with Ash, Ripley's big, floofy, gender-bending son. He thrived in his new home with his devoted humans and big sister Catsy and grew bigger and more dashing every day. Then, one day, a photograph appeared on his Facebook page of Ash sporting a new bow tie...

It was a hot summer night outside, but inside the casino, I was cool as ice. The roulette wheel was on my side and my pile of chips was steadily growing. I counted out another hundred and pushed them across the baize until they rested on number 8, black. My lucky number—reminds me somewhat of my mother, only without the ears.

I felt hot breath on my neck and a waiter leaned over my shoulder, placing before me a dry niptini—shaken, not stirred, two olives. Just how I like it. "Compliments of the lady..." he said.

I looked up and saw her, a stunning redhead draped in white furs, in spite of the heat. About her neck was a gleaming gold collar from which hung a single, brilliant diamond. "Eight carats," I thought. "Worth at least a hundred grand..."

Her green eyes surveyed me, taking in my immaculate tux and impressive whiskers—lightly curled with just a dab of wax for a subtle sheen—and my air of practised insouciance. I tweaked my bow tie a little and raised my niptini glass to convey my thanks. A half smile played about her lips and she tilted her beautiful head towards the door. I understood.

Draining my niptini, I cashed in my chips and bade my fellow gamblers a good night before strolling out to the lobby, where she was waiting. I introduced myself, although I had the feeling she already knew who I was. "My name is Bond. Ash Bond." "Oh, I know who you are, Mr Bond," she purred. "My name..." she extended an immaculately manicured paw, "is Pussy Galore."

"Please come with me." She began to walk towards the door, and then stopped, glancing coquettishly over her shoulder. "I'll make it worth your while...." I was intrigued, but my professional training had taught me to be cautious. Instinctively, I felt for my trusty Walther PPK, and then, flicking a stray ear tuft back into place, I followed her to her car. She drove fast and silently, as we snaked our way out of the town and into the foothills of the mountains. All my senses were on high alert as she steered the car towards what appeared to be the blank stone face of a cliff. As we approached, the whole cliff face rolled slowly upwards and we drove inside. A small door ahead of us slid open. Pussy climbed out of the driver's seat and opened my door. "This is where you get out," she purred. "My boss is waiting to see you."

I stepped through the door into a dimly lit room which appeared to contain nothing, save a large desk, behind which was a high-backed chair. The chair slowly swivelled round and I found myself staring into the impassive, pale face of a hoomin. His silver hair was swept back from his forehead and he sported a set of whiskers on his top lip which were almost (but not quite) as impressive as mine. The eyes behind the studious-looking spectacles radiated pure malevolence. On his lap sat a large and beautiful white cat, whom he stroked with great delicacy and tenderness.

"Greetings, Mr Bond." The voice that emanated was smooth and languid. I was impressed, especially as he hadn't appeared to move his lips. "How do you do that?" I asked. "Please don't play games, Mr Bond," said the cat. "We have business to discuss. Thank you, John. You may desist now." The man stopped stroking and sat immobile. "There is a chair behind you, Mr Bond. Please sit down." I sat, and immediately metal clamps pinned my limbs, front and back, and I was unable to escape. A familiar, immaculately manicured paw relieved me of my gun.

"Do you recognise this?" the cat continued, indicating a brown substance in a small dish. "Of course," I replied. "It's catnip." "Exactly, Mr Bond. The scourge of the feline world. The means by which the hoomins have manipulated us and subjugated us for generations!" "Oh, I don't know," I said. "I'm quite partial to a bit of 'nip myself—in moderation, of course."

"This is like no catnip you have ever encountered before. It has been genetically modified, so it no longer has any narcotic effect... "

"What's the point in that?" I asked. The cat's tail began to twitch. He did not like being interrupted.

"It no longer has any narcotic effect... on CATS. But on hoomins..." He cackled, a sound so evil that it sent a shiver down my spine. "Think of it, Mr Bond. The entire hoomin race enslaved to catnip! A new world order. The order of Felidae—our order! It will be we cats who will laugh while they chase little plastic balls and points of red light! It will be WE who shut THEM indoors at night! It will be WE who make THEM poop in public! It will be WE who take THEM to get..." he closed his eyes and a slow shudder shook his frame "...FIXED!" The last word came out like a hiss. For a split second, I felt an infinitesimal flash of empathy, but... Oh no! It could not be.

"We're not ready yet!" I yelled. "One day, maybe... but not yet. At least, not until we've figured out can openers!"

He sighed. "I was hoping you and I could work together, Mr Bond." He was icy calm now. "But, as it's obvious that we cannot, I'm afraid… this is goodbye." He pressed a button on the desk and the floor in front of my chair retracted, revealing a sparkling blue pool… and a heaving, and boiling mass of savage, razor-toothed fish. "However, I hate to dispose of an enemy before lunch. John, my napkin and my fork, please." He hooked the fish out one by one and ate them with relish (tomato, I think), spitting the teeth into a black onyx bowl.

As I watched in horror (tomato with piranha—what a faux pas!), I felt the brush of fur against my cheek and Pussy appeared in front of me. Bending down low, she whispered in my ear, "I can help you escape, but first you must do something for me… "

"Anything…" I breathed.

"Get your big butt out of my window seat."

Eh… huh… what?

"Owwww… Catsy! I was just getting to the best bit…"

Tall Tails 2: Make It So

In which Mythbuster kitten Jamie (now Rio) attempts to keep his unruly troops in line.

Space, the final frontier...

These are the voyages of the Critter Room Starship "Enterprise" (Captain Mordoc at the helm)

Captain's log, Stardate 2421.9. We've been over two months in the white nebula, and there is still no end in sight. Crew morale is at an all-time low and tempers are beginning to fray. Only this morning, my Science Officer bit me on the foot. I pray for an end to this featureless expanse and our return to blackness of normal space. Our time here has not been without incident, though, as these extracts from the ship's records will show:

Stardate 2421.1: We are imprisoned in some kind of alien penitentiary. I cannot see my shipmates and I am being force fed on some kind of rich nutritional supplement, which is keeping me subdued, so they can work their evil machinations upon me. I am awaiting the arrival of The Giant Claw, which comes every day to scoop me high into the air and dangle me over a chasm, before dropping me unfeelingly onto cold, hard metal. A mechanical voice spits out meaningless numbers, before the claw grabs me again and I am returned to my cell. However, little do they know that I am getting stronger. I will bide my time until I am ready to fight back. My crew will help me. We will prevail!

Stardate 2421.2: I regret to report that I have had to quell an insurrection led by First Officer Kayleb. He says that he is not an android. I informed him that he is a funny shape and therefore he must be. Failure to respect the chain of command incurs the most severe punishment, so I sat on him.

Stardate 2421.3: We have escaped the penitentiary. For some unknown reason, The Giant Claw has turned on its masters and thrown open the gates of our prison. We stumble gratefully towards freedom, leaving The Claw to battle to the death with its evil overlords. I fear no one will be left alive. However, the Prime Directive forbids us to interfere in the affairs of other cultures, which really is quite handy, because it looks really cool out here.

Stardate 2421.4: I have today had to put down another mutiny, this time by Science Officer Elinora, who demanded to know in a most insubordinate fashion who had put me in charge. I accused her of having ideas above her station and failing to obey a direct order from a superior officer. She made a rude noise and went and sat in the litter box.

Stardate 2421.5: Science Officer Elinora has been attacked by Klingons! She got one on her foot and managed to spread it all over the floor. I sound red alert as we all try to bury it.

Stardate 2421.6: The encounter we've been dreading the most since we left spacedock. Yes… (pause for dramatic effect)… THE BORG! I don't know how it got onto the ship unnoticed, but, as my head of security, Tactical Officer Shara will have a lot of difficult questions to answer. It was enormous and terrifying—neither man nor machine. It had cybernetic eyepieces and a strange sort of fibrous insulating material above its mouth, presumably to stop its face from catching fire. It came in among us but seemed to only want to observe us, and then it removed matter from our litter box, presumably so it can sample our DNA. Before it departed, I'm sure I heard it say "You will be stimulated. Sisters are futile." I am backed up in this by First Officer Kayleb, who says it might be an evil alien but it makes a good point, but the girls think I must've misheard. More insubordination! I will remove their holodeck privileges.

Stardate 2421.7: My Tactical Officer is sulking. I pushed her through the hole in the floor of the bridge, but I am the Captain and I can do what I like. I'll probably apologise to her later. The ship needs her Tactical Officer.

Stardate 2421.8: We have Trouble with Tribbles. Oh yes! Someone (ahem!) brought one on board without my knowledge. My Science Officer made a brave attempt to kill it but was obviously not successful, because now the place is littered with them. It should be the Tactical Officer's job to remove alien intruders from the ship, but sadly she is still not speaking to me. I was going to apologise to her for the hole incident, but I'm afraid I pounced on her tail instead. I don't know what came over me.

Stardate 2421.9: Today. I have to go—Mum wants to talk to us. I have a feeling we're about to boldly go where no kitten has gone before.

Thanks for joining in.

KARI'S VALEDICTION

Some words of wisdom from a mother to her growing children, who are soon to set out into the wide world without her.

So, my children, the time we all knew was coming has finally arrived. You are on the threshold of your greatest adventure and we must all be brave and look to the future. Because what a future it's going to be! This is the last time we are all going to be a family and we will probably never see each other again, but that is the way it has to be. Our time together is just the first step down the long road of our lives. It is time to pack up our things and move on.

Tomorrow, you will be taken into the homes of hoomins. Good hoomins, like the ones we have encountered here and you will enter into the pact with them that will sustain your lives, and theirs, for the rest of your days. They will provide you with shelter, warmth, food and safety, as well as companionship and love. But you must keep your side of the bargain too.

My two boys—your role is to bring joy and laughter, comfort and sustenance to your people. Their lives are complicated, I have discovered, and they have many cares and troubles. It is for you to lessen those cares, to lighten their load, to wish them a good day when they leave home, and to be their joyous first sight when they return. Be strong for them and keep watch over them. Learn their moods and know when to respond with a purr, a murr, or a knead of the paw. And remember to pursue the red dot at all times. Without fail. This makes them happy.

My two girls—you will be so beautiful when you grow up. Teach them your beauty and patience and tolerance. Share with them your wisdom, your tranquillity, your peace. Be their playmate in the good times and their rock when things are bad.

All of you—the gifts you have: your eyes, ears, noses, cheeks and tails, your purrs and your paws. Remember to retract your claws and soften your mouths and don't forget to sing to them that all is well during the night time. Hoomins are creatures of the daylight. They are afraid of the dark, so they will appreciate this. Remember too, to leave a little piece of yourselves on all the things they touch, to remind them that you love them. You were endowed with fur for this purpose.

Enjoy the rest of your kittenhood. It should be full of love and fun and games. There will be no responsibilities placed on you, so make the most of this golden time, for it will soon pass. But, girls, remember to count the turns of the Moon. When she has turned twelve times, listen for me. I will be calling for you from the Great Circle.

So, let us move over here where the watchers cannot see us, and say our last goodbyes. Let us touch our paws together and take The Oath—the one I have been teaching you. It is not to be taken lightly. Think about the things we pledge and take them forward into your new lives. Now, let us touch noses.

Goodbye, my darling babies. I am so proud of you. Be strong tomorrow and every day after, and remember to look forward to the future with excitement, not back to the past with sadness. I will miss you so much, but I know you are going to be extraordinary. I love you all.

Mafdet's Journey

More news of the Great Circle, cat lore and legend and an introduction to two extraordinary Critter Room mothers: Glados of the AI Fosters and the legendary Rosemary.

Dark of fur, and golden eyed, the young she-cat sat, paws tucked under her, dozing lightly in the late afternoon sun against the wall of a suburban house, no more than a shadow amongst the dark green leaves of a garden shrub. It wasn't her house... she didn't belong there. She belonged nowhere in particular. As the sun went down, she dreamed... dreamed of a cool, dark space in a hot, hot land far from the place she called home. She dreamed of the same place most evenings and often, as she patrolled her territory in daylight, she looked for it—or somewhere like it—but had never found a place that even remotely resembled it.

The sky darkened and the temperature dropped. The cat shook herself awake, sat up and looked up at the sky. The Moon was still low on the horizon and not yet ready for communication, so she passed the time making her customary greetings to those of her ancestors who were already visible. She located The Great Cat's Eye and looked across to where Old Tom lay on his back, sleeping away eternity. She loved to look at Old Tom. She imagined him to be a big old red cat, fat and contented, but still wise and kindly, like the old boy she had met behind the seafood restaurant. He

20

had invited her to shelter from the rain and had shared his bowl of fish heads with her and told her all about his youth as a ship's cat sailing the Caribbean Sea. She hadn't believed his stories, of course, but she was far too polite to say so to a generous cat who had shared his meal with her. And anyway, the stories were fun. She left Old Tom to his infinite slumber, and scanned across until her eyes alighted on the faint cluster of tiny stars that made up The Kittens. Seven of them. She hoped it wasn't going to be seven… Finally, she found her favourite constellation, the Diamond Collar. Yes… she would look good in a diamond collar…

By now, the sky was alive and sparkling with the eyes of her myriad ancestors looking down upon the world. It was a significant night for the young cat. The Moon had turned twelve times since her birth and the days had gone from long and balmy to short, cool and wet and back again. Today was the day she left her kittenhood behind forever and she was in need of guidance. She had never been afraid of being alone in the world. The Lady Moon had guided her often and Her wisdom had kept her safe. But now, things had changed. She was no longer going to be alone, and those that were coming would need her protection. The Moon was high now and She was looking the young cat squarely in the face so, glancing quickly around to ensure that she was alone, she began to sing her question. And, on this special night—just as her mother had predicted—The Moon sang back.

"Listen…"

She had expected a little more than that, to be honest. However, one did not ask Her Ladyship for guidance only to ignore it once it was given, so she moved herself to the top of a wall where she believed she would be able to hear… whatever it was… a little better. After a while, during which she could hear only the wind and the usual sounds of the hoomin world humming through the night, she rested her head on her paws and drifted into sleep. She felt the heat of a blazing, noon sun on her back and dust beneath her paws and heard the sound of voices and the chink, chink of hammers working rock and a low, low rumble which she couldn't identify... she jerked awake and lifted her head. The rumbling sound wasn't part of her dream. It was real, but very faint and very distant. She listened intently, swivelling her ears to catch more of the sound. The rumble resolved itself into the murr of a cat, a long, long way off... and the cat was calling her by name. Startled, she responded, keeping her voice as quiet and low as possible. "Hello...?"

"Welcome... " said the distant cat, "... to the Great Circle".

It was a thrilling night. She had heard of The Great Circle, of course. Most cats knew of it, though not all were immediately invited to participate. There were many smaller, local networks who preferred to keep to themselves, but, in times of crisis or great celebration, all she-cats were welcomed in. She was excited to be able to talk again to her mother and her sister and she heard news of her brothers. She listened while the Circle exchanged news, gossip, information and some surprisingly filthy jokes. Emboldened by her joy at reconnecting with her family, she contributed the story of the rat in the drainpipe and was relieved when they laughed, despite having messed up the punch line a little. Then, the atmosphere turned more serious and a hush fell over the circle. Each cat was invited to give thanks to Her Ladyship for something or someone who had made their lives a little better during the month (she chose the red tom who had shared his dinner with her) and then many of the sisters gave the names of cats and favoured hoomins who had recently been taken up. They were properly commemorated, and their eyes were identified in the night sky, and named. It was a touching ceremony, and she felt a lump rising in her throat as she listened, even though she did not recognise any of the names. The Circle seemed to break up into smaller groups after that—friends sought out friends, family members got together, and she found herself in conversation with the cat who had first called her name.

"Your name is interesting," the far-off cat said. "Why were you named after an Ancient Egyptian deity?"

"I've no idea. There is a naming tradition in my family, going

back generations. My mother is named Ubasti, as was her mother before her. My sister is Pakhet and I am Mafdet. Many in our family have had the same names. Where is Ancient Egypt?"

"Ancient Egypt was a hoomin culture in which cats flourished. They were considered sacred and were protected and worshipped. The goddess Mafdet was a slayer of scorpions and snakes. She protected the Pharaoh's palace and she protected the sacred temples, where the hoomins worshipped. She was also a goddess of justice and retribution."

"I like the sound of her. I often dream that I am in a hot and dusty country and I am catching scorpions and snakes. They try to sting and bite me, but I slay them easily with my claws. Actually, I've never seen a snake or a scorpion in my life."

"Well, you see, we cats have two types of memory. There is the memory you keep in your head, of your life since you were born, of family, friends, enemies, places, favourite meals, best naps... and then there's the memory you carry in your bones. Those memories are passed down through so many generations that nobody can now remember where they originated. They are the echoes of your ancestors and they tell you who you are and where you came from. They also tell you how to be, how to think and what to do—provided you interpret them right. They are the very core of who you are. There were cats living in the temples of Ancient Egypt, keeping them free of vermin. They were revered and venerated. Maybe you are descended from an ancestor who guarded the halls of Mafdet's temple."

"How do you know all this?"

"Easy," said the far-off cat. "My hoomins have this machine. I've figured out how it works. Tells me all kinds of stuff... Anyway, have you made a decision as to where you're going to birth your kittens?"

"I asked The Moon for guidance," said Mafdet, plaintively, "but she just told me to listen. I don't know what to do."

"She told you to listen to us, for no one can advise you better than your own kind. You have a choice. You can take your chances living wild in the city and hope to find a warm, safe place to raise your family, and hope to find enough food for yourself and them by hunting and scavenging, or you can put your faith in hoomins. Life in the hoomin world can be very easy, very rewarding and very comfortable... if you find the right one, of course. We can guide you, and make sure that you do. You will be safe, warm, well-fed and loved, and so will your babies. I found a happy home in the hoomin world, by putting my faith in one man in particular. If you look up and to the left of The Great Cat's Eye, you will find a constellation of eleven stars and, near it, another of four stars. I myself named these The Father and The Son as a tribute to the hoomins who saved me and set me on the path to happiness. If you choose to do so, and if The Moon and the Fates are smiling on you, you may find the real father and son on earth. Then your future happiness will be assured. However, it is up to you. Now, if you'll excuse me, my daughter has recently joined The Circle, and I am anxious to talk to her before the sun rises. Think carefully, young Mafdet, and choose wisely."

"Wait…" said Mafdet. "You never told me what you dream about, and I don't know what your name is…"

"I have filled my head with many things since I was your age, so my dreams are often full of calculations and machine designs and star charts. But… sometimes, I see a dark forest in a northern land, with a cold, running stream from which I am drinking…" she tailed off and was silent for a while, before she shook herself out of her reverie. "I go by the name the hoomins gave me these days, because it is who I am. It's a warm and friendly name and I like the way it sounds when my people speak it. I am Rosemary."

The two cats bade each other good night, and Mafdet jumped down from the wall and once again took up her position amongst the plants next to the house. Her head was buzzing with the excitement of the night but, as the dawn came up, she began to doze…

She was walking through a cool, dark space… on either side of her, great columns rose, columns covered with intricate, carved patterns. There was a fine dust beneath her paws. On her lips, the taste of a recently consumed rat. She walked on, past a tall plinth on which stood a gleaming, black effigy of a handsome, fine-boned cat. Suddenly, the cool hall was behind her and she was outside in heat and blazing sunlight. All around her were hoomins, shouting, laughing, chipping at slabs of rock with tools, carrying bundles, cooking over small fires. As she walked on, every hoomin she passed bent down to stroke her head, or tickle her chin, some even lifted her up and spoke to her with affection in their voices. One offered her a small fish from his cooking pot, which she did not refuse. She came upon a small, clear pool and, bending her head to drink, she saw her reflection for the first time... a slim, long-limbed cat with large ears and fine, high cheekbones. Her coat was black and glossy and shot through with silver. Her almond-shaped eyes were the colour of the sun and... yes, she wore a diamond collar.

Mafdet awoke suddenly to the realisation that the sun was sinking once again, and that she had slept through the whole day without eating. It was hunger that had woken her up. She stretched and emerged from her hiding place, to find herself face to face with an unknown tabby cat.

"The Circle sent me to find you." said the tabby. "Have you reached a decision?"

Mafdet smiled. "Yes," she said. "I know now where I belong."

"In that case..." said the tabby, "...follow me. Your journey home is about to begin."

HOLLY'S SLEEPLESS NIGHT

A tale written at Halloween 2013. Glados and her family were in residence in the Critter Room, but we all remembered with affection, and a little sadness, Honey, who visited us for a short time before crossing the Rainbow Bridge.

In the middle of the night, when the room was quiet and the kittens were slumbering in a heap, Holly's ear twitched twice, and he opened an eye. "Hal... leave me alone..." he mumbled. There was no answer. He opened his other eye and lifted his head and saw, to his surprise, that his brother was fast asleep. Holly rested his head on his paws and closed his eyes, but found he was unable to go back to sleep. He tried using his brother Jarvis as a pillow, then he tried using his brother Eddie as a pillow then he tried turning round and round to find a more comfortable spot on the blanket. One rotation, two rotations, three... and he suddenly found himself staring, at point blank range, into a pair of blue, saucer eyes. He blinked. Above the eyes there were furry ears. Below the eyes there was a leathery nose and the neat, white whiskers of a kitten—a kitten he had never seen. "Hello," said the kitten. Bewildered, Holly looked over to where his brothers lay asleep. He counted. Hal, Eddie, Jarvis... they were all there. "Who are you? Have you just got here? Did they bring you in a box?" he asked.

Holly heard a sound like a tinkling bell as the new kitten laughed. "No." she said, "I've been here lots of times." "Why

27

haven't I ever seen you then?" Holly demanded, but the kitten was off, scampering across the floor in pursuit of a pink soccer ball. "Play with me!" she called, from the other side of the room, and swatted the ball at Holly. Half-heartedly, still a little baffled, he batted it back, but the strange kitten was no longer there to receive it. "Whaaaaa… Chickenfish!" She dived into Chickenfish, paws outstretched, and ran round and round the room with the toy wrapped round her waist like a corset, giggling all the way. Suddenly, she was in front of him again. "Don't you want to play with me?" she said, sounding a little sad. Holly put his head on one side. "OK, but you've got to tell me who you are and what you're doing here." "I just want to play," she said. "Let's have a game, and then I'll tell you where I come from."

So, the two kittens played. They rushed around the room, they dived in and out of Fishbed, they swarmed up and down the Tardis, they pounced on the mice, they pounced on each other, they wrestled, bit and bunnykicked and they had a fine old time. All the while, the little kitten giggled and squealed in delight and the room seemed to be filled with the sound of babbling streams and birdsong and the scent of meadows in the summer. And Holly's brothers slept on, undisturbed. Finally exhausted, the two kittens flopped down in the middle of the floor. The strange kitten began to vigorously wash her paws. "You promised…" said Holly.

She stopped mid lick, back foot still stuck up in the air. "OK," she said. She stood up and walked towards the window. "Come over here. Look out there, and tell me what you can see." Holly sat up on his back feet and craned his neck as far as he was able. He had never really noticed the window, nor what lay beyond it before. His whole world up to that point had been the cosy room, his family and games of chase and tag with his brothers among the toys and towers. Stretched up as high as he could go, he saw the expanse of black behind the glass, and the million tiny, sparkling jewels strewn across it. He drew in his breath. "It's beautiful," he whispered. "It's where I live," said the little kitten. "I've waved to you before, but you've never noticed me... you're it!" She whapped him on the nose and bounced off across the room. Unable to resist his exuberant new playmate, Holly gave chase. She was fast and she was agile. She swerved, turned, spun and doubled back and, however hard Holly tried, he was unable to catch her. She stopped suddenly and hunkered down flat on the floor, front paws splayed out, claws extended, her tail lashing. Her huge eyes sparkled with joy. "Now I chase you!" she squeaked, and off they both went again—up the towers, through the tubes, crashing side-on into the fences.

"Holly, what are you doing?" his mother's head appeared above the rim of The Enterprise. He stopped in his tracks and sat down. "We were just playing," he replied. "We?" Holly looked around and was surprised to find himself alone. The room suddenly seemed very empty and very silent. Holly's eyes filled with tears. "Where did she go?" he wailed.

Glados hopped down from the tower and sat beside her smallest son. "She went home," she told him. "That's all."

"So you saw her?" Glados nodded. "She said she lived up there... How can she live up there?" asked Holly, gazing through the window.

"Well, you're probably a little young to understand all this, but we cats believe that we live on earth nine times. There is no way to predict how those lives will be... Some may be long, some short, some difficult, and some comfortable. When those lives come to an end, as they all do, we cross over a huge bridge to a happy place full of soft beds, good food and good companions, until our time comes to return to earth once again."

"Are there games and toys?" asked Holly,

"Yes, there are games and toys too. At night, we can look down on our sons and daughters, and their sons and daughters and see the whole of the earth laid out below us like a huge carpet, and our eyes are visible to those down here as stars in the night sky. Sometimes, earthly lives are cut very short. Nobody knows the reason; it is just the way of things, so some of the stars you see in the sky are the eyes of kittens, no older than yourself. And, as you know only too well, sometimes kittens don't do what they're supposed to, and some like to come back to earth to find new friends. This doesn't happen often, but sometimes a very strong-willed kitten will defy the rules and come down in search of a friend whose will is as strong as theirs, for only the toughest and bravest will be able to see them and not be frightened."

"I wasn't frightened," said Holly.

"Then you are, indeed, the toughest and bravest of kittens", said Glados, smiling.

"But I'm sad for her," said Holly, his eyes filling up again. "She never got to play in the rings or in the Tardis or to go to sleep in the Chickenfish or to lie upside down in the big hands and play with the mousies, or..."

"Shhh…" Glados booped his nose. "There's no need to be sad, little one," she said, nodding towards the star-filled sky. "Look at how many friends she has up there…" Holly tried to count them, but got lost after five. "… and now she has you, too."

"Will she come to play again?" Holly began to brighten. "I'm certain she will, sweetheart" said his mother. "Look, she's saying good night to you." Against the dark sky, one star sparkled brighter than the others. It shimmered, it glittered, it winked three times, and then it faded. "Now, come and lie down with me and get some sleep."

Holly lay down, his back against his mother's stomach. She reached round and licked her little boy's ear, "Goodnight, Holly," she whispered. As Holly drifted into sleep, he thought he heard the tinkling of a tiny bell in the distance.

"I like Holly," said the kitten. "We had fun."

"I told you you would," said Glados. "And I promised him you'd come again."

"I will." she said. "Ummm… before I go, can I snuggle with you for a little while?"

Glados reached out with her paw and drew the little kitten towards her until she lay, a warm, purring bundle, tucked against her chest. She licked the little woolly ears affectionately.

"Goodnight, Honey," she whispered, and closed her eyes.

ON THE PASSING OF PETER

This little piece was written to mark one of the more significant events in the life of the Critter Room, the death of a tiny kitten called Peter, who passed away in John's hands after only four days of life. A short life, but one that was to inspire an unprecedented outpouring of generosity and creativity among the followers of the Kitten Cam.

Tonight we sing to the Moon.

Come to your windows, come out to your gardens, your yards, your balconies, your roofs, and your walls. Put the word out to your families, friends, and neighbours. Everybody is welcome, mothers and sons, fathers and daughters, for tonight the Great Circle is coming together to commemorate and celebrate the life of a tiny kitten whose time on earth was too short for Her Ladyship to have named him, but who was called Peter by those hoomins who knew and cherished him.

Welcome, Miranda and Ellie-Marie, Rosemary and Ripley, Laika and Kari, Hazel, Glados, and Dory and all of your children, for you have a special connection with this little lost one and his mother. Let us send our thoughts to Janine tonight, to comfort her and to give her strength to nurture the little ones who still need her. We will call her into the circle soon, when the time is right.

Look up and to the left hand of the Lady Moon. There is the group of stars we call The Queen, which is the manifestation of the great she-cat who protects and cares for those who have crossed The Bridge. She will have sent an emissary to the end of The Bridge to greet the one who is coming, for he should not start this journey alone and friendless. Soon, as the sun goes down and the sky blackens, we will see him arrive and we will name his star and he will twinkle and glitter in the night sky as he plays with his new friends.

And we shall also turn and seek out in the sky the two constellations which our sister Rosemary named and added to our pantheon a year ago. They are the ones named The Father and The Son. We will bow our heads and pay homage to the good, wise and compassionate hoomin for whom The Father is named, for he did his best for Peter and he will continue to do his best for Janine and her boys, and his best is very good indeed. His praises have been sung in The Circle many times before, but tonight we also send our love and our strength, for this is not an easy situation for hoomins to accept.

But first, let us sing to the Moon in praise of little Peter, whose life was so short, but so full of potential. He will live on in his brothers and his mother and in our memories and our hearts. And he will play among the stars and watch over his family and the hoomins who cared for him.

Look—the stars are fully out now and Peter is arriving, to sit beside our little friend Honey and to look down upon his family with love. Janine will understand all of this soon. And, maybe, so will the hoomins. His star is named. He will never be forgotten.

AT THE BRIDGE

We encounter Honey and Peter once more, living a very different kind of life. This story also includes cats and kittens from John's own household, Margo's Menagerie and Tinykittens. But it is Peter's tale.

"Honey... wait!"

"Keep up, slowcoach... we don't want to miss them."

"But I'm smaller than you... my legs are only little."

Honey sighed and sat down to wait for her small companion. Huffing and puffing, Peter finally caught up and sat down beside her to catch his breath. "Where are we going anyway?" he asked.

Honey was play-pouncing in the grass, where a tiny moth fluttered just out of her reach. "You'll know when we get there," she called to him, "Come on!"

The two kittens resumed their journey. Honey trotted in front, her head high, her step full of purpose. She was oblivious to all distractions and, apart from the occasional pause to sniff a flower or to swat at a loose leaf or to chase a butterfly or to laugh at the reflection of her own eyeball in a dewdrop, she remained resolutely focused on her goal. Peter scampered and cantered behind her, filled with anticipation and determined not to fall behind.

Just off the path, a bush rustled loudly and a marmalade kitten shot out in reverse, tail poofed, and a daisy in his mouth. "Mfff ghhth..." he said.

"Jean Luc?" said Honey.

The marmalade kitten spat out his daisy. "I thought I'd take some flowers with me, you know... to present to him? They fight back, though."

He left the lone daisy, a little chewed, on the ground and bounced off after Honey. Peter thought for a second, and then gently picked the flower up in his teeth before setting off at a run to catch up. After a short time, during which they did not waver from their purpose, apart from a short excursion up a tree, a pause to drink at a small pool, a few moments spent happily splashing each other with water and a comfort break for all three on a patch of soft earth, they came to a small stand of silver birch trees on an area of fresh, spring grass. The intense green was shot through with the gold of the late afternoon sun as it broke through the leaves and made dancing patterns beneath the kittens' feet. So intent were they, though, on reaching their destination that they hardly spent any time at all darting after the shadows, giggling and seeing who could jump the highest to reach the young leaves on the lowest branches. Peter thought this was the most beautiful place he had ever been. He loved the brightness of the colours and the warmth of the sun on his back and the smell of earth and new grass and the velvety softness under his paws. He could not stay, though. They continued walking until, finally, they broke out of the trees and emerged into the clear space beyond, and Peter drew in his breath at the sight before him.

The soft, springy grass continued to the edge of what appeared to be a deep canyon, dark and mysterious despite the sunshine. In front of him, right against the precipice, the gnarled trunks of two ancient trees twisted and knotted together to form an archway and beyond... was it a road, a path...? No, it was a bridge. A bridge that curved upwards and away from the cliff. A bridge so long that its span seemed to disappear into a silvery mist, which sparkled slightly as it swirled around in the breeze.

Still more magical to the little kitten, though, was the fact that this whole area—right up to the tree arch—was full of cats. He had never seen such a gathering. There were old cats and cats in their prime, long haired cats, short haired cats, curly haired and even hairless cats, cats of every hue and shape and size and many, many kittens. They sat, stood, loafed, stretched, washed, played, chatted, and dozed. They purred, murred, mewed, miaowed, chirped, chirruped, snored, and sang. Honey and Jean Luc were already seeking out friends and playing amongst the kitten pack, but Peter was overawed, until a familiar face appeared in front of him and booped his nose.

"Hello, Auntie Sheba," he said, a little relieved.

"How sweet of you to bring a flower," she said, "Although I think you should put it down for a while, or it might wilt." He laid the daisy carefully in front of him. "Did Honey tell you why we're all here?"

"No... is it a party?"

"Kind of," said Sheba. "We're here to greet new friends. They'll be crossing The Bridge tonight, so we need to make them welcome. Do you remember the night you arrived here?" Peter nodded. "Do you remember how you were feeling as you crossed over The Bridge?"

"Yes," he replied. His eyes misted up for a second at the memory. "I was sad because I'd left my mama and brothers behind, and I was scared because I was on my own."

"Exactly," said Sheba. "The new cats and kittens who are coming will be feeling the same way. They too will have left behind family and friends and hoomins who loved them and they are feeling very sad and confused right now. So, we come to The Bridge to meet them, so they can begin their new journey in the company of friends, just like you did."

"I don't remember so many…" said Peter, gazing over the multitude. He recalled his own journey across The Bridge, confused and lonely, missing his mother and brothers and his cosy nest. Even though there were other cats making the crossing with him, each of them was focused on their own feelings of loss and their apprehension about what awaited them at their destination. Each of them walked alone through the shimmering mist, eyes fixed straight ahead, lost in their own thoughts. Peter rarely allowed himself to recall that long, sad walk.

He much preferred his next memory, which was of emerging from the mist into a strange land lit by moonlight, a velvet sky scattered with a million jewels, a warm breeze carrying the tang of summer meadows and distant oceans and… a round, fluffy kitten face with huge blue eyes, neat white whiskers and a laugh like the tinkling of a bell… He remembered his sadness dissolving as the laughing kitten kissed his nose and licked his ear and scampered off to show him where the best climbing trees were and how he could shake the branches of a bush to make a cloud of butterflies emerge... Honey had been his big (and bossy) sister ever since and he adored her.

"Keep your flower safe," said Sheba, "and go and play until it is time. When the sun goes down, the Circle on Earth will meet and sing to the Moon to help our kitties on their way, and then we will be ready."

"Why do they sing?" asked Peter.

"It's the way of cats. The Circle is the whole community of cats all over the world, and when a cat or kitten reaches the end of its life, the Circle sings to the Moon, so that She will know of their passing and be ready to receive them and so that She will know of how they spent their time on earth, who they loved and who loved them. The song is sung everywhere—beneath the clear skies of the desert, in the Land of the Midnight Sun, in the icy dark where the Aurora dances, in the heat and thunder and lightning of the tropics, amongst the noise and grime of the city... everywhere. When the song finishes in one part of the world, it is picked up in another and continued as the Moon makes her way around the Earth. It is an endless circle, like birth, life and death. A life is lost but, somewhere, a new life begins. The song never ends."

Peter looked over to where Honey and Jean Luc were playing with the other kittens. He had loved listening to Sheba, even if he didn't understand everything that she said. Instead of joining in with the play, he sat on the cool grass and watched as the clouds turned from white to pink, all the while dreaming of deserts and auroras and thunderstorms. As the sky turned to deep indigo, there was a noticeable shift in the atmosphere. The hubbub ceased, sleeping cats awoke, chatting cats became quiet and there was a ripple of movement as they all formed themselves into a semi-circle. The air was alive with anticipation and Peter was almost beside himself with excitement, shifting from foot to foot, and eager to know what was going to happen next. Sheba sat down next to him. "Ok, Peter," she whispered, "back straight, whiskers forward. Here they come."

The mist on The Bridge began to ripple and swirl and shimmer in many different colours, then out of the fog stepped a handsome black kitten. He paused tentatively on The Bridge before stepping off onto the grass. Behind him came another young cat, black and white. Jean Luc ran forward to greet him and Peter watched as the two frantically washed and groomed each other, clearly overjoyed to see each other. Now, all around him, cats were walking forward to greet the newcomers as they stepped off The Bridge. All the meetings seemed to be reunions of family members or old friends, full of affection and familiarity. Peter wasn't sure what he was supposed to do. There would be no friends or family of his coming tonight—he had looked in on his family earlier that day and they had all been fat and healthy and happy as usual. He looked back at the handsome black boy who had been first across The Bridge. He was standing alone, looking sad and confused. Remembering how relieved and safe he had felt the moment he had been greeted by Honey, Peter at last knew why he was there.

A firefly danced in front of his nose. Trying to focus on it made his eyes go crossed, so he eyeballed it with just his right eye. "I pounce you later," he hissed. "I'm busy right now."

Peter stood up, straightened his back and stiffened his whiskers then, clutching his daisy, he stepped forward towards the black kitten.

TRUFFLES AND TAPS

This little piece was written for the family of Truffles, auntie and mentor to Grant and Tory of the Mythbuster Kittens. Taps was a Tinykitten, brother to Calypso's Dancing Kittens, who was stillborn, but still deserved a future.

"Hello, tiny kitten. Who are you?"

The grey cat stopped mid-wash, and lowered her back foot to get a better view of the small, dark creature who had appeared in front of her.

"I don't know."

"What do you mean, you don't know? You must have a name."

"If I have, I don't know what it is."

"Wait a minute... don't go anywhere..."

The grey cat closed her eyes for a few moments. When she opened them, she peered closely at the tiny kitten.

"There, it seems you do have a name after all. They gave you one just as you were crossing the bridge. The hoomins named you Taps."

"Really, why would they give me a name?"

"Because they're hoomins. They're the best of hoomins too. They wanted to give you an identity, so they would remember you, even though they would never know you."

"I wish I could have met some hoomins. I never had the chance. Did you meet any?"

The grey cat closed her eyes once again, and a slow smile spread across her face.

"Oh yes, I knew hoomins... I lived with two special ones, and six other cats. I was known as the quiet one... every group has a quiet one, right? And, for a long time, I was the only female. That meant I represented my brothers at the Circle, asked questions for them, interceded for them, asked Her to keep them safe and to watch over them... it was I who sang to the Moon for all of us and She was good to us in return. I loved my Sammy and that big, benevolent old carpet, Loki, and I watched with pride as my Preston and Tucker grew into handsome, kind and generous young men.

And then, the kittens came. I was a little upset about that at first. We had our lovely, settled family who all respected me and knew that I liked to watch quietly, away from the noise and activity and now, two rambunctious kittens were brought into our midst unannounced, with no manners whatsoever, crashing around, climbing my cat tree without so much as a please-excuse-me... but, you know, those two kittens were so pure in spirit, so innocent and so loving that I warmed to them in spite of myself. And they were funny... oh, they made me laugh so much... they were like a fresh breeze blowing through the house. Everyone was rejuvenated by their simplicity and their sense of joy. I came to love them, in my way. I loved to watch Grant and Tucker becoming best buddies (such similar personalities), and I would laugh to myself as gentle, patient Loki sighed, rolled his eyes and made room as young Tory squashed herself into his sleeping box to suck on his fur.

It was a pleasant life. The hoomins moved around our world as if it were their own. They were gentle and kind and they knew exactly how much I liked to have my fur ruffled and to be scritched behind the ears. They kept my pink comb for me and laid out the warm blankies and they allowed me to watch, from across the room, the great hoomin pastime of Hockey, in which many hoomins chase a small mouse around a slippery floor with sticks then, when one hoomin catches the mouse, all the others try to eat him. I later had the great pleasure of teaching the rules of this game to Tory, who is now an avid fan, even though she sits far too close to the screen. She says it is the hoomin version of the mysterious red dot, only more violent. That little lady has wisdom beyond her years.

Of course, my favourite time of the day was crunchy time. It was just a little supper snack, but I would listen—quietly, of course—for the rattle of the biscuits on the tin bowls, and Tory and all the boys would dash to the kitchen and I would follow on, with far more dignity, and all the bowls would be in a row against the wall and we would each have our own and we'd line up... the snacks were lovely, but less important than the feeling of safety and companionship I got when we were all together like that...

So anyway, I have taught young Tory all about the Great Circle and how to sing to the Moon and how to keep the boys in line and she will be my successor and I know she will keep them all as safe as I did. Once her first year had passed and she was old enough to take on the responsibilities, I knew it was time to go. I said my thank you's and told them I loved them in the only way I knew how and I think they understood..."

The little kitten looked wistful. "It sounds wonderful. I wish I had some hoomins..."

"If you didn't even get a first chance at life, you will be able to go back very soon. That is how it works. You will find your special hoomin. I know it."

"What about you? What will you do? Will you go back?"

The grey cat rolled onto her side and, stretching out her legs right down to the toes, yawned languidly.

"I expect so, one day. But, for now, I'm going to rest here. I plan to find a nice sunny spot where I can cook all down one side, then another where I can cook all down the other side and I shall enjoy my memories as I bake. Then, when it gets dark, I will lie on my back and count the stars at the same time as I count my blessings... and you know what I plan to do at crunchy time?"

"What?"

"I'm gonna have crunchies..."

The Ballad of Rosie and George,
Part One: Meeting

It is a well-known fact that every follower of the Kitten Cams retains a special place in their hearts for their first mama cat. Mine was Rosemary, mother of the Spice Kittens, way back in 2012. After she had been in her forever home for about a year, her humans decided to adopt another cat to keep her company. Some of us were dubious—the imperious Rosemary sharing her home, her toys, her space? Little did we know...

In the beginning, the Sun and the Moon met to divide the world between them. The Sun took the land, the Moon took the oceans, the Sun took the daytime, and the Moon took the night time. The Sun took gold, the Moon took silver, the Sun took life, and the Moon took death...

Then they had to divide up the living things and this was difficult. They discussed and they argued and they debated and they cogitated, and they decided to divide the living things of the world into two, so each would take half. Both were happy, until they came to consider the cat. Both the Sun and the Moon wanted to have guardianship over the cat, for she was truly the most beautiful living thing to walk the earth. They quarrelled long and hard over the cat.

The Sun said, "She is such a beautiful creature and her fur would glisten beneath my light and she would luxuriate in my warmth and her eyes would shine like emeralds and all the other beasts would have the opportunity to feast their eyes on her wonder, which they could not do if she were only to walk at night."

And the Moon said, "She is swift and lithe and she can pass silently through the world. She is a wraith, a spectre, a shadow who glides on feet of air, unseen, unheard. She is clever and resourceful, she lives on her wits and she can bend all other creatures to her will with just a flick of her tail or a glance from her emerald eyes. She is truly a daughter of the night and she belongs to me."

The Sun had to admit that she had a point. He agreed that the cat truly belonged to the Moon, but he exacted a high price for his sacrifice. The Moon had to give up the flowers and the trees, the birds and the butterflies, the beasts of the field and the fish in the oceans (all bar a few, which he didn't really want). But she was happy.

She had the cat.

Rosie: I love that story. The Sun got the best deal on the face of it, he got all the fields and the forests and the gardens and most of the birds and animals and the hoomins, of course, but the Moon got all the interesting creatures. She got bats and rodents and bush babies and owls and foxes and badgers and moths… and us, of course. And, because she wanted us above all other creatures, we worship her as our mother and our protector and guide. She watches over us all and our ancestors sit with her and watch over us too. I know my nana is up there looking down—I have found her eye in the night sky—and all the others who have crossed The Bridge too… that is why I love to sit and look at the stars and to study them. They are my favourite subject to talk about at the Great Circle. I love to study and learn. It gives me something to do when my hoomins are not awake.

What is the Great Circle? It is the way we she-cats communicate, one to the other, in an unbroken chain. We teach, we learn, we discuss, and we debate. We swap news of friends and family, we send comfort to the frightened, the sad, and the lonely. We encourage those whose journey is just beginning and we commemorate those whose journey has ended. We search for the missing and guide home those who are lost. Nothing is hidden from us. And we get to gossip, as well.

I just came from the Circle. It's my favourite night—I get to chat with my daughter and all the other girls. Most of them share their homes with other cats. Lots of those cats join in the circle too—Ripley has her Lilly and Luna, Lacey brings Tucker, Glados is with one of the boys she raised, and young Tory has recently joined now that dear Tuffy has crossed The Bridge and she lives with a whole army of boys. They all seem to be happy to share. I couldn't imagine it. Sharing my hoomins and my toys and my blanket—nope, can't imagine it.

George: Bad day. I have no idea where I am. I've been bumped around in a tiny box, hauled out by my scruff, stood on a cold table in a bright and shiny room. I've had strange hoomins put their hands all over me and twist my ears and prise open my mouth and peer at my teeth and at one point they stuck something sharp in my bum... yowzah! Now I'm in another box. It's a bit larger and at least there's a warm blanket and some food and water and somewhere to pee. Too tired to think about it at the moment. I'll try to figure this out after I've had a nap. Naps solve most problems, in my experience.

Rosie: Are you a lion or a tiger? I have researched with interest the lives of our larger, wilder cousins and I have been surprised at some of the things I've found out. The tiger is a fabulous beast—

huge and handsome, secretive and solitary. She lives alone in the forests, seeing no one and needing no one, hunting by night and only meeting her kind when the urge comes to breed. Sometimes, I have dreamed that I am living alone in a dark forest, keeping to the shadows and living by my wits, hunting for meat or hooking fish from a cold stream. I have always believed that I was, by nature, a tiger—independent, resourceful, self-sufficient. The lion, on the other hand, lives on the open plains, where there is no cover or protection. She lives in a group with her extended family, hunting together, babysitting each other's kittens, grooming each other and basking together in the sun, secure in the knowledge that the group will protect them from danger. I always thought there was a certain appeal to this kind of lifestyle, the comfort and comradeship, the feeling of protection and safety, waking up from a sleep to see a loved one nearby... but I never saw myself as a lion. No... I am a tiger. I function at my best when I am alone. Absolutely I do.

George: You know the saying "you can't teach old dog new tricks"? Well, you can certainly teach an old (well, adult anyway) cat new tricks. I'm still in the big box, and there's no way out, but I've learned the art of "working it." According to my neighbour, it's what you have to do if you are of the more... ahem... homely persuasion and you don't want to live in a box for the rest of your life. I've seen the kittens going home with hoomins, bless them—and that makes me happy. I couldn't bear the thought of those innocent little souls being cooped up, never experiencing the sheer joy of running just for the hell of it, and hiding just so you can leap out and pounce the next thing that passes. But I've also seen many, many cats who can only be described as "mature" being selected by hoomins—in fact, only yesterday, my neighbour himself was packed up in a box by two large and two small hoomins. They all seemed so happy... So, I carry on working it. I approach with confidence, I do my little chirrup, I head bonk the bars of the cage, I look them squarely in the eye and yell "TAKE ME HOME!"—nah, not really. I do all this, even though I would sometimes like to sit at the back of my cage with my face to the wall, wishing I was somewhere else. In general, I'm a very upbeat sorta kitty, but this place gets to you in the end. Don't get me wrong, I am fed well and I'm comfortable and the hoomins are very gentle and kind but... the view never changes—three cage walls and the tabby across the way washing his nethers... I want more than this. Anyway, here they come—teeth 'n smiles, Georgie boy... teeth 'n smiles. Hang on, weren't these two in the other day?

Rosie: Ssshhhh! Not now! Something's going on. Not sure what. Lots of activity... new bowls... new toys. Surely they won't. Would they?

George: So... I'm going home. I'm not sure what that means exactly, but the signs are good. My hoomins seem like good 'uns and they were certainly impressed by my working it because, homely or not, they picked me. ME! I'm trying to act all calm here by lounging around in this moving box but my tummy is all in a knot. You see, my hoomins (MY hoomins!) smell, like so many of them do, of lilac bushes and cut grass and pine forests but, underneath it all, I can detect just the faintest wisp— the merest waft—of a she-cat. Could be trouble, or could be heaven. I'll just have to bide my time and try to be patient. Just realised I've been gnawing my own toes for the last ten minutes—ouch! Calm, George... calm...

Rosie: As a cat, my eyes are remarkable. I have a reflective layer behind my retina which improves my night vision, as well as making me look just a bit scary if someone shines a light in my face. I have a 20 degree greater field of vision than most hoomins so I can detect the smallest movement out of the corner of my eye and I do not need to blink to moisten them, which assists me by enabling me to focus long and hard and track small prey in the grass. Add to that the fact that they are delightfully almond shaped and the most beautiful shade of leaf green, and I can honestly say that my eyes are one of my best features. However, they are totally incapable of seeing anything through the slit around the bedroom door, however long I sit here with my eye pressed up against it. But I can hear him and I can smell him. I know he's in there. I KNOW he is…

George: Oh my! This is a turn up for the books. I've been shut in a room on my own—it's a million times better than my box before— clean litter, good meals, fresh water and a whole bed all to myself… I've been properly scent marking my hoomins, but I couldn't help noticing a certain she-cat was doing the same… between us, we've pretty much overwhelmed the scent of lilacs and pine, but the hoomins don't seem to mind. Then, the other day, they opened the door just a crack—and there she was. A goddess. That silken fur, those emerald eyes, those luxuriant paws and… that tail! I can only dream of having a tail like that—like a high cirrus cloud on a summer's day. And… her face—full of intelligence and personality— even when contorted into a hiss. I can't help noticing she has wonderful ginger chops, just like me. I've always thought they were my best feature, but on her… Yes, I am smitten. Last night, she came to the door and we whispered to each other. I understand that she is a little shocked at my sudden arrival, and she was quite clear in laying down her ground rules—no stealing her food, the left-hand tower is hers, the blue kicker is hers, if I lose a mousie under the fridge and need it retrieving, she does the talking… but I think— I hope—we can become friends.

Rosie: Oh my! This is a turn up for the books. He's been shut in the spare room on his own for a while, but now he is out and walking around my territory. What shocks me is the fact that I don't mind. He steps carefully, and respects my space. He smells a bit funny, but I think I did too when I first arrived. He isn't handsome as such, but he has a friendly face and twinkly, laughing eyes. And I can't help noticing he has wonderful ginger chops, just like me. I've always thought they were one of my best features. He's lacking in refinement and sophistication, but that is just down to his lack of education. I can deal with that. I am a natural teacher. I will teach him about the stars and the Moon and about cat lore and history and also vital life skills like how to kill a feather on a stick and how to cheat at the whack-a-mouse game. I have even told his name to the Circle, and commended him to the Moon so she can watch over him. I've told him who's boss round here, of course, but I think—I hope—we can become friends.

George: Was life ever not like this? Did I ever walk the streets at night and scavenge for scraps? Did I ever get into fights over morsels of rancid meat and have stones thrown at me for straying into the wrong garden? Or has life always been this, warmth and safety, a full belly, a choice—an actual CHOICE—of comfortable sleeping spots, loving hoomins to teach and an extraordinary and beautiful feline to learn from? She is a wonderful teacher, so full of learning and insight. Sense of humour too... I love to make her laugh. I am indulging our she-hoomin by letting her teach me to sing, which cracks Rosie up and I do it just for the joy of hearing her laugh. She has gradually allowed me to introduce her to the joy of sharing a sleeping spot—the warmth and softness of another body, the comfort of hearing someone breathing close to your ear and feeling a heartbeat under your head. She said it reminded her of the days when her kittens would pile on top of her and they would all sleep in a warm, twitchy heap for hours. She, in return, has been showing me the true meaning of cleanliness, especially around the ears. She doesn't know how much I am comforted just knowing she is in the house with me. For a long time, I couldn't believe they wouldn't load me back into the box and take me back to the boring cage, where I would have to "work it" all over again, but she convinced me that all is well. "You're family now," she said.

Rosie: Make yourself comfortable on the window sill or the small tower, so you can see the night sky to the north. Tuck in your paws and look up to where you can see the Great Cat's Eye, the star that shines the brightest. You see, all the stars form patterns in the sky, and we give those patterns names. Now, look to the right of the Great Cat's Eye, you will see nine stars which resemble a cat lying on its back with its paws in the air—well, that is called Old Tom. In the centre of those nine stars is a little cluster of seven stars, very faint. They are called The Kittens. Now, straight above the Cat's Eye, you can make out a pattern of seven stars which might just suggest to you a fish, which is called The Fish (I never said the names were original, lol) and, below and to the left, a semi-circle of eight stars which we call The Diamond Collar. The stars were named long ago by the thinker and philosopher cats of Egypt and Greece and the knowledge has been passed down from mother to daughter, father to son. But it would seem that, once upon a time, humans could understand the language of cats, as I have discovered that they name the stars too. Surely this tradition can only have been taught to them by our ancestors. There are two shapes in the northern sky which they call Ursa Major and Ursa Minor, the Great Bear and the Little Bear. They put me in mind of some humans I once met, so I have added them to our pantheon and named them The Father and The Son. I hope this will serve as my tribute to the kind humans who comforted me when I was confused and frightened and built a lovely warm den for my little ones and me. All the other stars, they are the eyes of our ancestors who have passed over The Bridge and are waiting for us on the other side. There is my nana, third star along at the right-hand of the Moon, and there are your granddad and your little lost sister next to him... George, are you OK? Your eyes have gone all misty... Come and sit next to me so I can baff your ears. You know, maybe I am more lion than I thought...

George: Move over, then. I can't fit on here with your enormous, floofy butt in the way. Turn a bit sideways... and shift your paw so I can at least park my posterior; not sure these towers are really built for two handsome beasts such as ourselves.

Rosie: Ach... stop fussing. There's room for the two of us wherever we need to be. Now sit still while I tackle these massive jug ears of yours.

George: Ooohh... that feels good. Raspy, but good. A bit to the left please... Are we OK, Rosie?

Rosie: Yes, George. We're OK.

TALL TAILS 3:
THE TUXEDO KNIGHT'S LAMENT

The magnificent Ash makes another appearance, this time inspired by a caption added to a photograph on his Facebook page.

I'll sing you the song of brave Sir Ash
The Tuxedo Knight, who cut a dash
Through every village in the land
And set himself to win the hand

Of a toothsome maiden, pure and fair
With eyes of green and auburn hair
But a heart of stone and will of steel
Before whom lovelorn knights would kneel

To no avail, for to win her heart
Her knight should be a man apart
And prove to her that he's the best
By embarking on a reckless quest.

So brave Sir Ash, the Tuxedo Knight
A handsome cat, but not so bright
Agreed to do as she desired—
A confrontation was required...

So, as the dawn rose in the East
He rode out to slay the Gnarly Beast
With no assistance, save his page...
His groom, his cook, his mystic sage,

His favourite hawk upon his sleeve
And don't forget his best mate, Steve,
A guard, in case of stealth attack,
His favourite mousie in his pack

A hundred cans of Fancy Feast
A pound or two of 'nip at least
His water bowl and fluffy bed
A pillow for his weary head...

But, three hours out, down came the rain
His entourage went home again.
And, left alone, in God knows where
His maiden didn't seem so fair.

His voice cried out in pained remorse
"I can't believe I'm on this horse!"
The beast stopped still and turned her head
"I'm not so thrilled myself," she said

"Now, where is it you want to go?"
He had to admit, he didn't know.
"I've never seen the Gnarly Beast,
Where does it sleep, where does it feast?

I have to think this quest has failed,
I'm soaking wet and my crew has bailed.
They've taken all the food and 'nip,
I'm going in here to have a kip."

He walked inside a cavern's mouth
He yawned and stretched, then headed south,
But, in the middle of the night
He was woken by an eerie light.

The Gnarly Beast was standing near
It sensed his shock, it smelled his fear
He drew his sword and stood up tall...
He didn't fancy her at all.

She dropped her dinner down her dress
Her red hair was an awful mess
Her conversation made him bored
She couldn't play the harpsichord...

The Beast drew near, its eyes aflame
With foul breath that could stop a train.
He stared into that ravening maw
And held up a defensive paw...

The Beast struck out, its jaws held wide
And sucked the hapless knight inside
And as into its throat he slid
He thought, "Steve owes me fifty quid..."

He raised his head, all bleary-eyed
And looked around and peered outside.
No talking horse, no beast to battle,
Instead the skyline of Seattle.

The clink of plates, the smell of meat,
It's time to find himself a treat.
He knows that, in reality,
"The only ravening beast is me..."

STORY TIME

We fans are always grateful when adopters decide to set up Facebook pages for their new family members, and even more grateful when these pages are updated regularly. It enables us to keep in touch with the kittens and mothers whom we have grown to love and it also introduces us to new and extraordinary characters, who become part of the Kitten Cam landscape. One such character was Loki—gentle giant, loving uncle, random yak...

He hadn't known what to expect. He knew he would probably meet cats to whom he was probably related and cats he had spoken to through the glass or from inside the tunnel of sun and rain, and cats he had heard of through the Great Circle. He hoped he would meet one or two of the famous cats he had held in high esteem for their wonderful singing voices, their awesome beauty or their legendary hunting skills. And he knew he would be reunited with a beloved friend. The reality took him completely by surprise, though. As he stepped off The Bridge onto the springy turf (a feeling which he found slightly startling, though pleasant) he found himself face to face with a huge crowd of cats of all sizes, shapes, colours and ages—there was just a sea of faces, all smiling, with their eyes fixed firmly on him. And the noise! It sounded like distant thunder rolling over the mountains and it kept on rolling—into his ears, his paws, his whiskers, and it grew louder as the crowd of purring cats began to walk towards him. As they came close enough, each of them either touched his nose with theirs, or extended a paw, or pressed their bowed head against his, and then moved on. He sat, a little taken aback at this outpouring of love and respect until, gradually, the crowd dissipated and he could actually see some daylight. And that is when he saw her, sitting a few feet away from him, smiling and blinking away a small tear.

"Tuffy..." They touched noses and licked ears and bonked foreheads, and he gazed into the familiar, beloved grey face and was forced to stifle a sniff. "I've missed you. We've all missed you," Tuffy smiled and gave her old friend an extra lick on his woolly ears. Life was sweet on the far side of The Bridge, but now it was just a little sweeter.

The sun was setting as the two friends strolled side by side through the birch glade and onto the path that led away from The Bridge. Loki's senses tried to take in all the new sights and scents—

there were so many—the smell of fresh grass and newly cut hay and pine trees and lilac blossom and the distant, salty tang of a far off ocean, the rosy glow of the setting sun reflecting on the silver bark of the birch trees and the tiny dancing shadows cast on the grass by the leaves, the loud rustling, squeaking and whispering, accompanied by the occasional glimpse of a furtive kitten face popping up from behind a stone...

"Why are all those kittens following us?" he asked.

"You're famous," Tuffy replied, "And I don't think they've ever seen anything quite like you before." She stopped and gave a low murr and, slowly and tentatively, kittens began to emerge from behind every rock, tree, bush, and hillock. As their walk resumed, they found themselves at the apex of a flying wedge of over-excited kittens and young cats, all bursting with pride at being allowed to accompany this magnificent creature to his destination.

"Where are we going?"

"To the meadow—for story time."

"Oh good—I love stories. Who's telling them?"

"You are..."

He cleared his throat, nervously surveying the audience ranged at his feet, and shuffled a little on the molehill on which he stood.

"I'm sorry," he began, "But I don't know many stories. In fact, I only really know one—my own, so I hope you'll forgive me if I stick to that." The audience all hunkered down contentedly, tucking in paws and curling up tails. He cleared his throat once more...

"I was lucky enough to live in a castle. It was a true fortress, keeping us safe from the dangers of the world outside. With me lived a handsome lord in a black velvet cloak, a venerable grey lady and two young squires. We were also lucky enough to have two of the most faithful, loyal and useful hoomin retainers, who hunted prey for us, prepared our meals, kept us well groomed and provided us with many comfortable places to sleep. We wanted for nothing and our happy home remained unchanged for some time. Then, one day, one of the young squires (I forget which) came running in to tell us that he'd found two urchins lurking under the desk and they wouldn't speak to him and refused to come out. Well, I found this hard to believe, so I went to see for myself and—sure enough—when I bent down and peered with one eye under the desk, there were two pairs of eyes peering back at me. 'Who are you?' I asked. 'Who are you?' replied a set of eyes. 'What are you doing in there?' I asked. 'What are you doing out there?' replied the other set. I sighed. It was going to be a long night...

"Eventually, the hoomins were able to persuade the urchins to come out from their hiding place. We all took a good look at them, sniffed them carefully and voted almost unanimously to keep them (Sammy voted against—he was afraid they would eat all the crunchies). So, despite the fact that they smelt a bit funny and had no manners to speak of, they became part of the household. For several weeks, the halls of our castle rang to the sound of thundering kitten paws and the crash of falling ornaments, and occasionally the squeaks of protest as one of the young squires decided that a bit of chivalry was called for and cuffed an urchin round the ear. I would take refuge in my favourite sleeping box for a bit of peace and quiet, but it would be only a matter of minutes before the small she-urchin would push herself in beside me and keep me awake by sucking noisily on my fur. I found this most bizarre, but Tuffy told me she was just missing her mama, so I tolerated her and I soon found myself warming to this odd little creature.

"The he-urchin, in the meantime, found many areas of common ground with the young squires, mostly food, destruction and sprawling on his back with his legs in the air. As time passed, we grew accustomed to their joyful presence, until we could no longer remember what life had been like before they came. They took on the task of keeping the castle walls safe from wild beasts, by glaring through the window at them, and Little Tory Longtail put herself in charge of checking our food, before it was served, for substance and quantity. She also began to spend more time with the grey lady, whose task it was to educate her in cat lore and the ways of the Moon and stars. Truffles, as the only female, was the household's representative and advocate at the Great Circle, a job of great responsibility which could not be undertaken by any cat without the necessary education and, although none of us liked to think about it, a time would come when Tory would be obliged to take on that role herself.

"That day came sooner than we expected—and long before I was ready. Our beloved Truffles told us it was time to say goodbye and I was so unprepared and terribly sad, not just to lose our dear sister and friend, but sad too that Little Tory Longtail's kittenhood was so soon over and that she no longer needed our protection. In fact, it would be she who would be protecting us and watching over the household, as Tuffy had done for all those years. Tory crept into my sleeping box for the last time that night and we were glad for each other's company, for the next day Tuffy set off on her journey to The Bridge.

"So Tory sat in the window in the last hours before dawn and sang Truffles' name to the Moon and we all listened as the song was picked up by every cat in the Circle. Then, in accordance with the tradition, we looked up and waited, and, sure enough, a tiny star appeared like a jewel in the night and sparkled brighter than the others and I thought, 'Is it her... is that our friend?' And I saw the star wink with an emerald light and I knew. Our sister was watching us now and she would watch us forever.

"And then, the time came when I knew I too had to leave and I asked them for their help and it was gladly given, even though it made them sad. And I said my goodbyes to the young squires and to my darling urchins and to my old friend Sammy and told them I would be watching over them until the time came to meet again. Then I said goodbye to my hoomins, which was much, much harder..."

He tailed off, unable to think what to say next. Tuffy licked the top of his head and pointed into the sky. All the cats in the meadow fell silent and looked up. It was a cloudless night and the silver crescent of the new moon (his favourite) hung low over the horizon. Then, as he watched, a small star appeared winking with an emerald light and, beside it, another, fiery amber like a topaz. It burned in the sky like the flare of a match and, on the breeze, he thought he could hear the echo of a familiar feline voice, singing his name. And all the cats in the meadow joined in the song, to give thanks to the Moon for the life of Loki.

Much later, Loki and Tuffy sat together in the meadow, tranquil and content. All around them were curled up cats and piles of slumbering kittens.

"Where do we sleep?" asked Loki.

"Anywhere we like," Tuffy replied, "But tonight I thought you might appreciate this."

She stood aside to reveal a battered cardboard box, and Loki couldn't help but grin. He climbed in and tested its construction (a little shabby—good) and size (just a little too small for his huge frame—perfect!) and he circled around ten or eleven times just to get the feel of it. Once he was oriented to his satisfaction—positioned so that he could see his new star if he chose to open an eye—he began to doze.

A small sound brought him back to wakefulness and he found, peering over the rim of his box, a small black kitten gazing at him with huge saucer eyes.

"Yes...?" he asked. The kitten said nothing, but continued to gaze at him. "Shoo... off you go. It's time you were asleep." The kitten's eyes began to mist, and her lip trembled a little.

Loki sighed deeply and rolled his eyes.

"OK... just for tonight," and he shuffled over to make room.

The Ballad of Rosie and George, Part Two: Parting

After too short a time together, we had to say goodbye to Rosie's devoted sweetheart, George. His departure was sudden and unexpected and he made his journey across The Bridge without having had the opportunity to say goodbye to his true love. But Rosie is not just an ordinary cat...

"But I never got to say goodbye!"

He stood stubbornly before The Bridge, looking back, unwilling to believe that his time had come to cross, afraid of stepping into the swirling grey mists that obscured his path, reluctant to leave it all behind.

"Walk with us, brother." Two black cats had stopped in front of him. "There's nothing to fear."

"But I've left my only friend behind. What will I do for companionship? Who will sleep beside me and tell me stories, and teach me about the Moon and show me the eyes of my ancestors in the night sky?"

"Come along. It'll be OK. You are expected."

There seemed to be no other choice so, dejectedly, he stepped onto The Bridge, flanked by the two black cats, and together they headed into the fog. The walk felt like an eternity to him. He could see nothing but grey gloom for a long time—he even lost sight of his companions, although he could feel their presence close to him. But still he felt alone—more alone than ever before, and the thoughts continued to tumble around in his head—why me? Why now? We had so many naps left to take, so many games left to play, so many things left to discuss...

Then, slowly, the mist began to grow paler and he became aware of colours dancing just on the edge of his vision and a twinkling like a million tiny shooting stars, and a tang in the air of new mown hay and a distant, salty ocean... then he stepped out into the pinkness of a summer sunset. Beneath his paws was the sensation of fresh, springy grass. Above his head a perfect sky of rose and gold and purple. In front of him, a small, unassuming grey tabby cat, who beckoned him to follow her.

"Hello and welcome," said the grey cat, as they made their way through a small birch copse and onto a rough path leading away from The Bridge. "I am Tuffy and I have something to tell you. Some of us are lucky and know when our time is coming and we are able to prepare, but some, like you, find themselves here before they are ready and they worry for those they have left behind. So, we arrange for them to have a little company crossing The Bridge, to allay their worst fears, and, sometimes, we can also arrange this..." They had stopped on a shingle bank at the edge of a wide, slow river. Around them there were stands of tall reeds and yellow irises, through which skimmed jewel-like blue damsel flies. Beneath the green water, he could see shoals of tiny silver fish darting between gently waving green fronds, and the reflection of the last rays of the sun as it sank below the horizon, briefly turning the water blood red.

"What are we doing here?" he asked.

"Watch the water when the Moon comes up. We will be waiting for you in the meadow."

The grey cat disappeared, and he sat down on the shingle and waited while the sky turned from blood red to purple and then to deep blue. He breathed in the cooling air, savouring the scent of earth and grass and the far-off salt tang. The inky darkness was suddenly pierced by a shaft of silver so bright that he briefly had to close his eyes. He looked down into the water just as the grey cat had instructed and there, shining and rippling and smiling up at him, was the face of the Moon. Maybe it was an illusion caused by the movement of the river surface and the sound of the breeze through the leaves, but he was sure the Moon was calling him by name. He bent closer to listen and, as he did so, the face of the Moon began to change, its edges became blurred and soft, the silver became white, and the shadow of a cloud began to resemble a pair of beautiful ginger chops...

"Rosie?"

"George?"

"Yes, it's me. I don't know how I'm doing this and I've a feeling we don't have long, but I wanted to say I'm sorry. I had no idea when I left that I would never be coming back. There was so much I would have told you if I had known."

"It's OK," said Rosie softly. "I had a feeling, so I sang to the Moon last night to ask Her to let us meet one more time."

"Wow! I can't believe She said yes. Does She owe you money or something, or is my Rosie more important and mysterious than she ever let on?"

"A little of both," said Rosie with a chuckle. "Oh, George..."

"Sshhh..." said George. "There is nothing you can possibly need to say to me that I don't already know. When I had nothing, no home, no family and no hope, somehow I found you. You taught me about wonders and mysteries beyond my wildest imaginings, you made me laugh until my sides ached, you soothed my sleep when my dreams were bad, you tolerated my terrible singing, you kept my ears quite ridiculously clean and, above all, you gave me happiness that I never in my whole life thought I deserved. Our time together may have been short, but it was rich and full and I was a better, wiser and more contented cat because of it."

"And you, George, you showed me that a kind heart and a generous spirit was more important than all the knowledge and book learning in the world. You reminded me to appreciate the simpler things in life, a shared joke, a good vigorous baff, a long nap on a rainy afternoon. I will never forget to appreciate those things, and I will never forget you."

"Rosie, my sweet girl—I want you to do two things for me."

"Anything…"

"Firstly, I know you will, but promise me you'll take good care of them and let them know how much I loved them. Secondly… would you tell me one more story?"

Rosie sniffled a little, before clearing her throat.

"A young lioness walked the plain. She strutted along with her head held high, confident that she was the queen of all she surveyed. She was afraid of nothing, for she was part of the pride and they protected her and kept her safe and gave her love and comfort and companionship. She had recently joined the hunt for the first time and she was proud that she had helped to bring down the antelope which they had all shared, and for once she had not had to wait until last before it was her turn to eat. So confident was she in herself that she had left the pride snoozing under a tree while she wandered far from home, because she wanted to find out what was out there. She saw ostrich and giraffe and antelope and wildebeest and a troupe of noisy baboons and she licked her lips at the thought of tomorrow's hunt and, better still, tomorrow's dinner. So preoccupied was she with her thoughts that she didn't realise she had stumbled right into a herd of huge buffalo. Now buffalo were the one thing she was afraid of. If buffalo ever wandered close to the pride, the young lions were under orders to scatter in all directions, so that none of them would become a target. But now she was alone, and all of the beasts were looking straight at her and snorting steam from their great nostrils. In a sudden fit of panic, she turned and ran blindly as fast as she could, with no direction or goal—anything just to get away. When she finally stopped, panting, she realised she had run into the forest and she had no idea where she was or how to find her way out. She turned this way and that, but every path looked the same. It was dark and full of strange scents and even stranger noises. Frightened and lonely, she lay down and put her paws over her eyes, trying to block out the unfamiliar sensations with which she was bombarded.

Day turned to dusk, and the lioness remained frozen with terror, until she felt the touch of a paw on her cheek. She uncovered one eye and looked up to see a she-leopard sitting in front of her, surveying her quizzically. "So, what is the mighty lioness doing in my forest, shivering with fear with her paws over her eyes?" "I'm not afraid!" retorted the lioness, still shivering, but not wanting to let her façade slip. "Yes you are," replied the leopard, "And what's more, you are afraid to admit you are afraid. That will get you nowhere. I would offer to help you, but if everything is under control..." "OK, OK! I am afraid. I am lost in this dark forest and I don't know how to get home. Everything here is so strange—there are terrible screams and shrieks, and awful, awful, smells, yet I can see nothing. I don't know if something is going to swallow me whole, or suck out my brains, or capture me and make me dance for them at their feasts..." The she-leopard laughed aloud. "Those sounds and smells are just the inhabitants of the forest going about their business. They are not at all frightening—mostly. Come on, I will show you how to get home." The two big cats set off side by side, pushing through the undergrowth, and the lioness noticed how the she-leopard would stop from time to time to rub her face against a small rock or the bark of a tree. "Leaving myself a trail," she explained, "so I can find my way home." "Aren't your family going to worry about you, away from home at dusk?" asked the lioness. "I have no family," replied the leopard. "I haven't seen them since I was a cub. It's the nature of leopards to live solitary lives." "Ooohh... I can't imagine what that is like!" said the lioness. "I could never be separated from my mother and my father and my aunties and my siblings. We do everything together. I feel so sorry for you—you must be lonely all the time. Maybe you can come and join our pride, and then you'd never have to be alone again." The leopard smiled and said nothing, and the cats walked on. Suddenly, the lioness squawked and jumped in the air. She had trodden on something squishy and squashy in the dark, and it had hissed at her. "What is it? Will it eat me?" she whispered. "Good evening, Mr Snake," said the leopard. "I apologise for my friend—what are you up to this evening?" "Digesting..." said the snake. The lioness noticed the huge, deer-shaped swelling in the snake's belly. "Eewwww..." she said, curling her lip. The leopard bade the snake a polite good evening, and they walked on. A sudden rustling in the trees made the lioness jump again and, looking up, she saw a small black and white face peering at her. "Good evening, Mrs Colobus," said the leopard. "How's the family?" "Keeping me busy," said the monkey. "The kids are into everything and now a family of chimpanzees has moved into the next tree—shrieking and yelling at all hours—I never get a wink of sleep…" "Sorry to hear that," said the leopard. "Tell you what—I'll have a quiet word with the chimpanzees. Maybe they will move to a tree farther away. In fact, I'm sure they will." The monkey thanked her and the cats walked on. All the way through the forest, the leopard greeted her neighbours and passed the time of day. They all seemed to like and respect her. The lioness was baffled. "But surely, these are the same creatures that you eat." "True…" replied the leopard, "But they know that. They understand that it is my nature to eat their kind, but they accept me for what I am and just hide around mealtimes." "We lions tend to stick together," said the lioness. "We would never think to make friends with a giraffe or an antelope or a zebra." "Well, perhaps you should change all that. I am a solitary creature, but I don't envy you your pride in the least. I embrace every species in the forest, and we help each other in different ways, each according to our own abilities." They walked on in silence until, at last, they reached the edge of the forest and the plain, vast and moonlit, stretched out before them. "Would you like to come and meet the pride?" asked the lioness. "Er… not now, thanks," the she-leopard replied. "I'm sure they'll be relieved to have you back and I'm pretty sure they won't want me getting in the way. Besides, I'm not sure they would accept me for what I am…" The lioness had to agree. "Probably not, but I always will." So, the two cats parted, each returning to their very different lives but, from then on, they met often at the edge of the forest, and they walked together and talked about their days, and the leopard learned about the plains and the lioness learned more about the jungle and they discovered what made them different and what

71

made them the same, and they were enriched by their relationship, which continued until the end of their days."

"It's only a little story, but it seemed appropriate," Rosie said.

"And the moral? There's always a moral..." said George, smiling.

"Friendship is where we find it. We might not have a big, stable family to back us up and provide us with love on tap, but if we go through life with our eyes open, and our hearts open and we are prepared to admit when we need help and to accept that others are different, there is love and support to be had all around us. We just have to embrace it. We found that out, didn't we, George?"

He smiled. "We certainly did. Oh, I'm going to miss you, girl."

"Me too."

"Don't ever stop watching the sky, will you?"

"As if... I'll be watching for your star tonight."

Loath though he was to tear himself away from those beautiful emerald eyes and that beloved face, he felt a pull that he could not resist.

"Rosie, I have to go."

"Yes, I know."

"Love you forever…"

"Me too…"

He turned to leave.

"George…"

"What?"

"We were OK, weren't we?"

"Yes, Rosie. We were OK."

And he turned his back on the river, lifted his head and walked through the trees towards the meadow, where a thousand friends he never knew he had were waiting to welcome him.

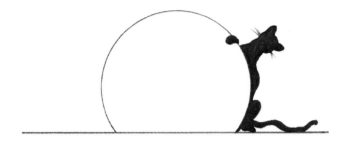

THE KITTENS THEY CAME IN TWO BY TWO

A small birthday song for FDJ (with apologies to whoever wrote "The Animals Went in Two by Two.")

The kittens they came in two by two
Hurrah, hurrah
The kittens they came in two by two
Hurrah, hurrah
The kittens they came in two by two
Their tails so floofy, their eyes so blue
And they all came into the ark, for to get out of the rain

The kittens they came in three by three
Hurrah, hurrah
The kittens they came in three by three
Hurrah, hurrah
The kittens they came in three by three
And Daddy John said, "You'll be safe with me"
So they all came into the ark, for to get out of the rain

The kittens they came in four by four
Hurrah, hurrah
The kittens they came in four by four
Hurrah, hurrah

The kittens they came in four by four
They marched right in and they closed the door
And they all came into the ark, for to get out of the rain

The kittens they came in five by five
Hurrah, hurrah
The kittens they came in five by five
Hurrah, hurrah
The kittens they came in five by five
So happy and lucky to be alive
'Cos they all came into the ark, for to get out of the rain

The kittens they came in six by six
Hurrah, hurrah
The kittens they came in six by six
Hurrah, hurrah
The kittens they came in six by six
With zoomies, pounces, and bunny kicks
And they all came into the ark, for to get out of the rain

The kittens they came in seven by seven
Hurrah, hurrah
The kittens they came in seven by seven
Hurrah, hurrah
The kittens they came in seven by seven
Peeing in Chickenfish feels like heaven
They all came into the ark, for the get out of the rain

The kittens they came in eight by eight
Hurrah, hurrah

The kittens they came in eight by eight
Hurrah, hurrah
The kittens they came in eight by eight
Nomming their way to their target weight
And they all came into the ark, for to get out of the rain

The kittens they came in nine by nine
Hurrah, hurrah
The kittens they came in nine by nine
Hurrah, hurrah
The kittens they came in nine by nine
All looking their best for adoption time
'Cos they all came into the ark, for to get out of the rain

The kittens they came in ten by ten
Hurrah, hurrah
The kittens they came in ten by ten
Hurrah, hurrah
The kittens they came in ten by ten
And so the cycle begins again
And they all come into the ark, for to get out of the rain

The kittens they come and come some more
Hurrah, hurrah
An endless queue outside the door
Hurrah, hurrah
The hungry, lonely, the lost, and stray
Not one of them will be turned away
So they'll all come into the ark, for to get out of the rain

THE DAY OF THE DEAD

A poem written to mark Dia de Los Muertos. The Babylon Five kittens were in residence at the time.

"Tell me again what I do with this broom…"
"You push it," said Susan, "to sweep up the room."
Uncle Kougra had told them to polish and buff
So they dusted and tidied and hid all their stuff.

"Tonight will be special," their uncle had said,
"It's the time when we gather to honour the dead.
So polish your whiskers and tuck in your vests
As we're going to play host to some most honoured guests."

The kittens weren't sure they'd be very good hosts—
Do you give snacks to zombies or drinkies to ghosts?
Do you tell jokes to vampires and—well, what the heck
Do you say to a guy with a bolt through his neck?

As the sun turned to red and the sky turned to flame,
The guests were arriving, by the dozen they came.
They were hanging up streamers and blowing balloons
And laying up tables with knives, forks and spoons.

There were platters and glasses and bowls and tureens
Filled with more food and drink than the kittens had seen.
And Spices and Ripleys and Clones and AI's
All gossiped and chatted, while watching the skies.

Then away in the distance, the sound of a bell
Rang the first stroke of midnight—a deep silence fell.
Then a breeze like a whisper, a change in the air
Like the breath of a ghost, and they were just... there.

There was Kari's lost baby and Holly's lost mum,
What a shriek of delight as Janine found her son!
And Tory hugged Loki and Tuffy kissed Grant
And Neil just kissed everyone—who says he can't?

And Rosie and George found a quiet place to chat,
While Peter and Honey attacked Zombie Rat.
And the Moon bathed the room in a magical light,
All together again, for just one special night.

Then Keaira and Sheba stole out of the door
To seek out the soul mate they'd lived with before.
And, leaving the others to party all night,
They jumped on his bed and they snuggled up tight.

What a party ensued—what a hullaballoo!
There was Musical Cat Trees and Poop-in-the-Shoe,
Pin-the-Tail-on-the-Vet and Squeak-Kitty-Squeak,
And enough games of Sardines to last for a week.

There was tuna and crab paste and kibble with dip,
There was ice cream and custard and big bowls of nip.
They munched and they slurped till the food was all gone
And then, as they relaxed, someone called for a song.

Kari stepped up and she started to sing,
But she had to keep stopping when Marcus joined in.
So Eddie and Holly, and Egon and Ray
Picked up their guitars and they started to play,

And the cats jumped and hopped to the sound of the boys,
And the room filled with laughter and colour and noise.
So they tangoed and jived till the furniture shook
All friends reunited, till someone said, "Look!"

Along the horizon, a grey misty light
Brought an end to the party, an end to the night.
So, softly and sadly, they said their goodbyes
And cuddled and hugged, brushing tears from their eyes.

And, in the dark bedroom, he started to stir
At the touch of a whisker, the sound of a purr.
And opening an eye—well he couldn't be sure
But it looked like a tail that just went through the door.

With a last glance around them, as night turned to day,
The dead and the living crept softly away.
And the kittens looked round them with shock and with awe
At the wreck and detritus strewn over the floor.

The carpet was ruined, the curtains were torn;
"He's going to be livid," wailed Marcus, forlorn.
But he cuddled the kittens and, smiling, he said
"It's the same every year on the Day of the Dead."

Happy Birthday Ghosties --
All Three of Them

This piece was written to mark the annual birthday gift drive, held to celebrate the Ghostbuster kittens' birthday and hosted by their humans for the benefit of Purrfect Pals. Of course, the third Ghostbuster brother is not forgotten, especially by mama Janine.

"Peter! I've been looking everywhere for you..."

Honey came bounding across the grass to where Peter was lying, sprawled on his stomach, peering nervously over the precipice into the void.

"I don't know why you look so nervous. You can't fall off," she laughed.

Peter slid back from the edge and sat up. "I dunno. It's weird. It seems such a long way down."

"What are you looking at, anyway?"

"Mum and my brothers. I always like to check in on our birthday, but I can't see them. The house seems to be full of boxes."

Honey leaned over and squinted through the mist. "Perhaps they've moved. Oh no—there's your mum, perched on the top of that pile by the stairs. Wow! That's impressive!"

"What is? Let me see!" Peter flattened himself on the grass again and slid himself gingerly to the edge. "Hold on—those are all birthday presents? What've those two louts done to deserve so many? I haven't had anything..."

"Don't be daft," said Honey. "Those gifts are not all for Ray and Egon. They're donations for the shelter. Remember, they did it last year too?"

"Oh, right..."

"And anyway," said Honey, "who says you haven't had anything for your birthday?" From behind her back, she drew a red balloon on a string, and a small cake, with two layers—one tuna and one chicken—slathered with fresh cream frosting. Stuck in the top was a small, burning candle.

"Happy birthday, Peter," she said.

"Thank you. How do I eat it?" He was entranced by the tiny candle with its dancing flame, but felt it was a little impractical to set a fire on top of food he was about to eat. His whiskers were definitely at risk.

"You blow the candle out." Honey told him. She'd done her research.

"But you only just lit it..."

"It's a hoomin tradition. You blow out the candle and make a wish. And don't tell me about it."

"Ah, I see." said Peter, not seeing in the least. He blew out the candle and made his wish.

"What did you wish for?" asked Honey.

"Hey! You told me I wasn't to tell you..."

She sighed—it had been worth a try—and handed him his balloon instead. He reached out a paw to grab it, claws extended to get a better grip on the smooth surface and, with a loud pop that sent them both scurrying behind a small shrub, it completely disappeared.

"Where did it go?" asked Peter, mystified, as his tail began to return to its normal size.

"I don't know," replied Honey, peering behind a rock, just in case. "Hoomin customs are weird. Better to just stick to our own. What did you wish for?"

Peter ignored this, and went back to watching his family. "They've grown so big," he said, a little envious.

"And handsome..." said Honey, which did nothing to allay Peter's envy. Life on the other side meant perpetual kittenhood, which was wonderful, but sometimes he wondered what it would be like to grow up.

He didn't ponder for long, as a rustling in the nearby bushes prompted him to look around. Heading towards him, bows round their necks and fancy hats on their heads, were about a hundred cats and kittens—all of his many friends. They were carrying toys and treats and platters of food and more cakes—no candles, sadly—and more balloons (he made a mental note to keep his claws tucked away this time), ready to start the best birthday party a kitten could ever want.

While they set everything up in the silver birch glade, laying out blankets and tables and hanging lanterns in the branches of the trees, he took one last look at the box-filled house, his big and— yes, he had to concede—handsome brothers and his beloved mama. Next to him, something caught his eye in the grass. The candle from the cake was alight again, its tiny flame dancing like a firefly. So, birthday wishes did come true after all...

He carefully placed the little wax stick with its dancing flame on a rock at the very edge of the void. "This is for all the lost and lonely kitties down there..." he whispered, "...a light to guide you home."

And down in the house, among the boxes, Janine gazed at the darkening sky. She knew exactly where to look—she looked every night—but on this one, she couldn't help but notice that his little star was twinkling more brightly than usual. "Looks like you're having a good party, darling," she whispered. "Happy birthday, Peter." And, blowing him a kiss, she hopped down and went to find her big (and handsome) sons.

The Choice

For some time, Peter and Honey had acted as our eyes and ears in the world on the other side of The Bridge. It was time for both of them to make The Choice... to stay, or to come back for a second chance at life?

Peter sat on a log on the fringes of the meadow and watched while Honey and her kitten companions chased each other in and out of the long grass, disappearing behind the tussocks and reappearing, laughing, sometimes bobbing their heads up above the stalks to get their bearings and to check whether their companions were within pouncing range. He smiled at their antics. It looked like a good game, and it was one in which he often enjoyed participating but, today, he was content to sit in the warm sunshine on the hollow log and watch.

He took a deep breath in. The air, as ever, carried the scents of new-mown hay, lilac, damp earth and that familiar, far-off salt tang. The sun was exactly as warm as he liked it—warm enough to heat the fur but not so hot as to sap the energy. Sometimes, he liked to bake under a hot sun, so he would just remove himself to where the sun was hottest. Sometimes, he had a fancy for watching the rain, and there was somewhere he could go to do that too. There were napping spots which were soft and napping spots which were firm. Indoor beds where he could be cosy and outdoor beds where he could lie and watch the stars. There was never any shortage of food—

which was the tastiest and most succulent food any cat could imagine, or water—which was as sweet and pure as nectar and could be sipped from any number of rivers, rivulets, streams, fountains, waterfalls, pools, and puddles.

In this place, there was no pain or sickness, no physical discomfort, no want or hardship, but there was still free thought. There was emotion too. Sometimes, someone would feel un-happy, or homesick for a past life, or they would feel the need for solitude or companionship and, for a kitten who overstepped the mark, there was discipline. Peter himself had often been on the receiving end of a squeak from an angry playmate or a cuff from an irritated adult. He had a way to go before he reached Honey's total though. That girl was incorrigible.

The game of chase had morphed into a giant bug hunt. He could see his friends spotting their targets, flattening themselves against the ground and shifting their weight from foot to foot in preparation for the deadly pounce. The bugs always got away. Honey was flying through the air, trying to bring down a dragonfly —which also got away—and laughing her tinkling laugh. There was rarely a time when Honey didn't laugh. Nothing seemed to dampen her high spirits.

Yes, life here was good. It was better than good—it was wonderful. But, every now and then, Peter felt a tiny tug in his heart that he did not quite understand. It had begun the night of his birthday party, when he had looked down to see his two brothers, now fully grown, sleek and handsome and so clearly loved by their human family, as well as by their own mother— Peter's mother. He had thought at the time that maybe, just maybe, it would be nice to experience life as a grown-up and to try out the actual growing up part, too. He had also thought that it would be nice to live alongside a loving human family. He had a faint, residual memory of his short time in a human household. He remembered the feel of a human hand, the sound of a human voice and now he was curious—a little. It was just a thought that popped into his mind every now and then, while sunning himself on a log, for instance, or sometimes just as he was falling asleep under the stars. The thought never persisted long, and it would disappear from his mind as swiftly as it had appeared, and he would go back to sunning himself or dozing without any worries... until the next time.

Honey came bouncing over to him, eyes shining, her grey fur stiff with burrs and a dandelion clock stuck to the top of her head like a fancy hat.

"Aren't you going to join in?" she demanded, trying to dislodge the dandelion clock with her back foot.

"I'm happy to sit and watch."

"What are you thinking about?" He knew by her tone of voice that "Nothing" was not an acceptable answer.

"Do you ever wonder what life would've been like if we hadn't—you know, come here?" he asked.

"Yes, of course," she said, to his mild surprise. "I think every-one thinks about it, especially we kittens. It's not the same as the old cats—they miss their old homes and their old hoomins, but at least they have memories to cherish. Us kittens never had that. We missed out on a lot."

Peter felt comforted to know that he was not the only one to ponder about what if. He stood up and stretched, a full arched-back stretch—standing up right on his tiptoes and turning his spine into an upturned U. That was the best sort of stretch. Feeling the muscles unwinding from his nose right through to his tail, he felt suddenly re-energised and leapt off the log and ran to join in the bug hunt, flattening, wiggling and pouncing along with the rest of the kittens. The bugs still got away.

Later that day, as the air began to cool and the sky began to pinken, they were making their way back along the path to where they knew they would find a good meal, a brisk baff from one of the adults—someone was going to have fun picking out those burrs—and the comfort of their companions, when they were stopped in their tracks by two cats who they did not recognise.

"You're wanted," said one of them, "back in the meadow."

The two kittens turned around, mystified, and headed back to the meadow where they had been playing moments earlier. When they arrived, they were startled to find a sizeable assemblage of cats, familiar and unfamiliar, all sitting round in a semi-circle. Their escorts ushered the kittens to a spot in front of the crowd and bade them sit down. They looked at each other, baffled and a little nervous.

"Don't worry," said a voice, "you're not in trouble for once." The voice belonged to Truffles, an old cat who had arrived after them, but who was treated with much respect by all the others. She was a quiet, polite lady but, when she spoke, others listened. She was accompanied everywhere by the enormous, shaggy Loki, who had been her friend on the other side and who was rarely far away from her. The kittens adored Loki. He was like a big, benign uncle who tolerated having his whiskers pulled, his tail chewed and trying to sleep with three or four of the smallest kittens snuggled up in his long fur, squeezing their tiny claws into his flesh.

"What's going on?" asked Honey.

"Well, for you and Peter, the time has come to make The Choice."

"What choice?" asked Honey.

"May I suggest," Truffles replied, firmly, "that you stay quiet for once and let the adults talk?"

Honey slumped a little, deflated, until she caught a glimpse of Loki's twinkling eye winking at her. Truffles began again.

"The Choice is offered to all who live here, cat or kitten, provided they have lives left to live. You will have heard it said that we cats have nine lives—even the hoomins have heard this, but they do not understand exactly what it means. When our earthly lives are over, we cross The Bridge and we live in this place, healthy and happy and with everything our hearts desire. The one drawback is that we never change over here. Kittens remain kittens, the old remain old. For some, this is a happy state of affairs, but for others—especially the young—it is unsatisfying. They often yearn for another chance at earthly life, to experience new things or to complete a journey which was cut short before. We all have nine chances to do that, to go back and I know you have both been thinking about it." Honey and Peter looked at each other, wide-eyed. How did she know? Had they been talking in their sleep? Best not to ask. Truffles went on.

"Please know that you are not obliged to return. You can stay here for as long as you wish. Forever, if you like, or you can choose to return later rather than sooner. However, the time has come for the two of you to make The Choice. You both have eight further lives to live and you can choose to do so the other side of The Bridge if you wish. Now, we understand that your previous lives were cut short very early and you don't have many experiences to draw on when trying to decide. So, some of our friends here have agreed to tell you of their experiences on earth. The one thing that is certain is that, if you return, it will be to the world of the hoomin. Listen to their stories and then think carefully about what they tell you of the hoomin world, its benefits and its drawbacks. Now, sit down and make yourselves comfortable. And don't interrupt..." she looked directly at Honey when she said this. "You may ask whatever questions you wish at the end... when there will also be snacks."

Still a little bewildered, but placated by the promise of snacks, the kittens settled down as instructed and prepared to listen.

A pale cat stepped up. She was one of the unfamiliar cats who had waylaid Honey and Peter on the path and only now did they notice how exotically beautiful she was. Her fur was the colour of cream, shading through gold to russet on her flanks and legs. She was tall and fine boned, with chiselled cheeks and a long, sharp muzzle. Her eyes were the colour of a setting sun and the shape of almonds, sweeping upwards towards her large, magnificent ears. She spoke in a voice like melted chocolate.

"My last life on earth was spent in a land of dust and sand, which lay parching under a blazing sun. Beneath the azure sky, the very horizon would shimmer in the heat and the eyes would be tricked into seeing things that were not there. In the middle of the day, the sand would seem to be transformed into a silvery lake, although there was no water to be found for miles. The air would be full of the whine of the relentless, hot wind, the strange echoes of the sand dunes as they shifted and the occasional, piercing shriek of an eagle as it scoured the land, searching for something—anything—to eat."

The kittens closed their eyes, transported in their minds to the burning, empty desert.

"Running through this land, however, was a great river. Every year it broke its banks and the land was flooded for many, many miles and it was this flood that transformed the fringes of this river into a fertile plain where plants and trees grew and animals and birds thrived and, naturally, it was ripe for exploitation by humans. They came in abundance and multiplied and cultivated their crops and raised their animals and built villages and towns and cities with great temples and statues. They had powerful kings who believed themselves to be gods and they had priests who grew fat by encouraging the kings to believe they were gods, but, for the people, life was good, food was plentiful and the climate benign and so a great civilisation flourished. These people, and their priests and their kings, had the good sense to include some animals amongst their pantheon of gods, such as the bull and the hawk and... well, let's face it... me.

I was born in a village outside the capital city, close to the site where many men laboured to build a great stone temple to the beautiful cat Goddess Bastet. I was one of many kittens, but it was the general consensus that I was the most beautiful. I was housed and fed by a stonemason and his family. It was he who was responsible for creating a great statue of the Goddess to stand in the hall of the temple on a huge sandstone plinth and, as I grew from kitten to cat, he made many images of me, using pigment made from powdered rock mixed with lamp oil. He painted me from every angle and in many poses, lying asleep, standing alert, sitting with my paws tucked under, but mostly he drew me sitting as I am now, my head proud and my eyes gazing towards the horizon."

By way of a demonstration, the cat sat neatly, paws together, tail curled round her feet, and then drew herself up so that her body formed a silhouette the shape of a teardrop. Lifting her chin, she gazed into the distance with a haughty expression. So noble did she look that Honey and Peter almost felt compelled to bow down in worship before her, but instead she relaxed, smiled and winked at the two kittens, before resuming her speech.

"When most of the fabric of the temple was complete, my stonemason set to work. He had shown the images he had painted of me to the priests who were overseeing the design of the temple and they had indicated their approval and so, taking a great slab of black basalt rock and his trusty wooden hammer and bronze chisel, he began to tap, tap, tap away at the stone. First he incised some guidelines to indicate a rough shape and then, with the aid of his two sons, began to chip away the unwanted surfaces until, gradually, little by little, a shape began to emerge from within. My shape. Over the course of many months, the three worked away at the stone, shaping and refining until, at last, instead of the crude black rock pillar, there stood a magnificent cat. She still needed to be polished smooth, and that task took several more months but, by the turn of the year, the statue of Bastet was ready to be moved into her final position inside the great hall of the temple. She was moved with great care by many men using wooden sledges, then ropes and pulleys. At last, our beloved goddess of love, motherhood, war, and justice stood upon her plinth, looking out between the columns of the great hall, towards the mighty river. There she stood for century after century, tended by priests and priestesses, visited in secret by many cats seeking aid or comfort, and worshipped by all who passed by the temple. Thereafter, the same image appeared over the years in infinite forms—in pictures, statuettes, jewellery... all of them me. I spent my life both as a humble but beloved house cat and as an object of worship for an entire civilisation. For me, earthly life could not give me more than that—any future life would only disappoint, my expectations having been raised so high, you see. So, I will not be returning. My future lies here."

The exotic cat bowed low to the two kittens and to Truffles before withdrawing into the crowd. They could still see her, standing as she did half a head taller than most of the others. Another, very different looking cat took up position in front of them. She was tiny, black and somewhat ragged. Her ear was notched and she sported scars around one of her eyes. Her tail had a sharp, angular kink towards its tip and her whiskers splayed in all directions. Her earthly life had clearly been very different from that of the temple cat. When she spoke, it was in a small, breathy voice that the kittens had to strain to hear.

"My last life on earth was on a small island in the north of Europe during what the hoomins refer to as the Middle Ages. It was a dark and primitive time. Most of the people were desperately poor and barely scraped enough from the land to feed their families. Most of the food they laboured to produce had to be handed to the local baron, so the peasants went without. They were oppressed by the nobility, oppressed by the church and oppressed by life in general, so I guess I can't really blame them for turning to superstition and witchcraft as a way to explain their lot. It was a bad time to be a cat. It was an especially bad time to be born a black cat. We were persecuted as being the familiars of witches, who were themselves considered to be the servants of the Devil. Many were slain by some terrible means in order to rid the world—so the hoomins thought—of evil.

My hoomin mistress was an old widow lady who lived in a hut made of dried mud and straw at the edge of a village on the eastern side of the island. It was a flat land of marshes and creeks where, even in the summer, the wind blew relentlessly from the sea, so that the trees and bushes grew bent over, as if they were trying to escape its constant howl. The local people toiled away digging great ditches to drain away some of the water so that they could cultivate the soil and grow grain and vegetables, even though most of these were given as tithes to the manor house and to the church. Ah... the church. It was a great building of men, which rose out of the flat landscape and towered over the huts and hovels of the peasants, as if to remind them daily of their position in the grand scheme of things. On Sundays, the whole village walked, limped, or shuffled in a convoy to the church to listen while the priests shouted hellfire and damnation at them, told them they would all go to hell for their sins and that they should repent their ways if they did not wish to be personally responsible for bringing about the Apocalypse. They even had to stand outside the church and peer in through small windows in the walls to be threatened and terrified like this. They were too lowly and insignificant even to be allowed through the doors. So ignorant and uneducated were they that they believed all of this and so tried at all times, out of fear, to do whatever they were told to do by those they considered their betters. It made me sad.

My mistress, though, was one of those who saw the truth. She did not attend the church, she did not pay their tithes and she did not fear God or the Devil. Unable to work the land due to her frail old age, she would dispense crude medicines made from herbs in exchange for bread and, sometimes, she would wave around a small bundle of bound hazel twigs and utter incantations for young women anxious to conceive a child, or to lure a certain neighbour's son into marriage. For this, my mistress received maybe a couple of eggs or some turnips. She would cackle quietly at the gullibility of some of her "clients," but at least she ate. Then, one night, a party of villagers arrived at the hut bearing flaming brands, which they used to burn the place down—we did not know why. Maybe one of the young women gave birth to a daughter instead of a son, or the neighbour's boy married someone from the next village instead, but thereafter we had to tramp the countryside together, barely surviving on the food she could gather and I could catch. She would still dispense her herbs and chant her incantations, but when she had finished, instead of receiving bread, the local children would run us out of the village, hurling insults and rocks at the same time. Crouched in the shelter of a hedgerow one freezing winter's night, she took me in her arms and said to me that her time had come to depart this earth, and that she was not afraid as the great Mother Hecate was waiting to receive her and would avenge her soul in this life and the next. I did not understand what she meant, but I did not want to be left alone in that cold and hostile world so, when my mistress uttered a last incantation and cast herself into the freezing river and I watched, with my own eyes, pale hands come up and catch her and bear her down into the depths— or maybe it was my imagination—I threw myself in after her."

The kittens were mesmerised and wide-eyed with astonishment and shock at the black cat's tale. Honey could think of a million questions to ask her, but she was still speaking.

"And yet, I have chosen to return. I had the misfortune to live in a hostile world, but I knew love from my hoomin who, I realise now, was unusual in that she could speak to me in my own language. But, anyway, I have faith that there is a better world to be found now and I wish to know the love of a hoomin once again. But maybe not a witch, this time..."

The black cat bowed and withdrew, leaving the kittens confused. "But..." stammered Honey, "...the cat who had the wonderful life wants to stay here and the cat who had the terrible life wants to go back..."

"Nothing is straightforward, you see," said Truffles. "You must follow your hearts. You will know if you have made the right choice, I promise. Now, I don't know about anyone else, but I'm starving..."

Confused though they were, the kittens' appetites were unaffected, and they tucked into the considerable spread with gusto. Loki sat down beside them, smacking his lips after consuming a plate of pilchards. Peter looked up at the big, shaggy cat and asked, "If we went back, would Honey and I still be together?"

"I don't think there are any guarantees," he replied. "If you opt for another life, you get what you get, if you see what I mean. The cats who spoke to you had experienced both extremes, good and bad. For most, though, life is more mundane. Take me and Tuffy, for instance. Our home was just an ordinary house, in an ordinary suburb, but it was better than the temple of Bastet to us, and our hoomins were just ordinary people who loved us—as we loved them, but they were better to us than priests or kings or witches. They made us happy, and I don't think there is any finer state on that side of The Bridge or this than to be happy. Tuffy and I don't need any other memories. The memories of that life are sweet enough but, maybe one day... who knows? You, on the other hand, have yet to acquire any memories. I can't imagine what that must be like." Loki turned his attention to washing his face and paws and the images continued to whirl in the minds of the kittens.

It was dark by the time the meeting broke up, and the Moon was on the rise. It was a warm night and the breeze was gentle and fragrant. The two kittens walked in silence to the place where they usually liked to sleep ignoring, for once, the fireflies that danced around their heads. Usually, they would find a good spot— a soft mound of grass, an indentation in the earth underneath a bush, or maybe a flat rock still warm from the sun, and they would settle down together and chatter, play and snooze the night away. On this night, though, they went their separate ways and each curled up alone—although still within sight of one another—both feeling that they needed solitude and silence in which to ponder the evening's events.

Peter lay on his back in the grass and watched the stars—there was his and Honey's, tiny diamond chips seeming to almost touch each other. There was Tuffy's emerald star and beside it Loki's amber one, there were Jaguar's and Siberia's sparkling like fire and Keaira's and Sheba's, soft like pearls... he idly wondered what happened to these stars if you went back. Did they disappear for a while, to reappear again on your return? He sniffed the scented air. Tomorrow would be another perfect day and he and Honey could spend it chasing bugs in the meadow with their friends if they wanted, or they could dip for fishes in the stream or climb trees or just bask in the sun, but... there it was again. That tiny tug in his heart, as if an invisible thread connected him to the earth on the other side. This was impossible! How did anyone ever choose? He yawned and rolled over, tired of thinking. It was unlike him to be unable to sleep, but something was keeping him awake... something not quite right. He heard a soft rustle in the grass beside him and felt a warm, familiar body—still a little lumpy with burrs—lie down close to his. The Choice could wait for now. They snuggled up and drifted into sleep

* * * * *

It was warm and dark in the nest, and safe. There was nothing to see, nothing to hear, just the comforting scent of mama and the soothing vibration of her purr. And nothing to do but eat, sleep and grow. Nothing to sense but the reassurance of another heartbeat close by... and the trace of a memory, faint, like a tiny star in the farthest reaches of space...

The young woman sat on the sofa, smiling as her son dangled the feather on a stick just out of reach of the kittens, giggling as they leapt into the air to grab for it before landing with a thud, feet splayed out on the wooden floor.

"He's good with them." the older woman said. "Not everyone is, but he's a natural. They're really comfortable around him."

"He loves animals," his mother replied. "He's just never had any of his own before. His dad wasn't keen, what with us moving around so much. But, now it's just the two of us..." There was a short silence which spoke a thousand words.

The boy was lying on his stomach, laughing as four of the kittens swarmed all over him, grabbing his hair and licking his face and ears. The fifth kitten hung back a little, preferring to play alone and he was chewing experimentally at the boy's sock, in the hope that it tasted like chicken.

"You know these four and their mother are already spoken for," said the older woman, "The only one still looking for a home is that little guy." She detached the small, cream-coloured kitten from the boy's foot.

"He's really cute," said the mother. "I'm surprised he hasn't been snapped up."

"Well, we encourage people to adopt in pairs, but when there's a litter of five, it means one will be adopted alone. It's a shame, but they usually adapt."

"Oh, he wouldn't be alone," the mother said. "We adopted another kitten about a month ago—it was on our application form. She's very sweet, but she seems bored and a little depressed, if that's possible. She sleeps a lot. We thought a playmate might cheer her up."

"Well, it would certainly cheer me up to think he would have a friend," said the woman. "What does your son think?"

"Do you like this little guy?" she asked.

"Well, he's not as much fun as the others," said the boy, "but maybe he's a bit overshadowed by his brothers and sisters. Let me hold him for a bit." The boy took the kitten in his cupped hands and lifted him up to his face. A pair of placid blue eyes looked into his. They looked deep into his. And they spoke to him. And he knew.

"If you don't want him, we can keep on looking," said his mother.

"No. This one's mine," said the boy, solemnly. "He told me so."

"Sometimes they do that," said their foster mother, and she was absolutely serious.

The women shook hands and said their goodbyes, and the boy clutched on tightly to the cardboard carrier containing its oh-so-precious cargo. In the car on the way home, he peered in through the air holes at its tiny occupant, who clung with all his claws to the towel at the bottom of the box, his eyes closed tight in fear.

"Mum, can I call the kitten after Dad?" the boy asked.

Involuntarily, she bit her lip. "Why would you want to do that?"

"I don't know. It's a nice name and it suits him, and... well, I think this kitten is special. He's going to look after us."

His mother smiled. "OK. I think he's pretty special too."

The boy peered into the box again and whispered to its little worried occupant, "Don't be frightened, Peter. We're going to have such fun!"

Late that night when the house was quiet, Peter the kitten sat alone in the small box room which was his temporary home. He had everything he could possibly need—bowls of food and water, a litter box, a scratching post, a comfy bed and lots of toys—but an odd feeling was keeping him awake. He felt as if, just maybe, he had been here before. Or somewhere similar. Try as he might, he couldn't make his memory stretch back further than the last ten weeks.

"Pssst..."

A tiny sound near the door caught his attention.

"Pssst..." There it was again. He went to investigate.

"Hello," said a muffled voice from the other side of the door. "Are you going to live here?"

"Yes," he said. "Who are you?"

"I live here too. I can't wait to meet you—it's been a bit lonely here on my own." A small grey paw appeared beneath the door, so he pressed his own against it.

And there it was again. The trace of a memory, faint, like a tiny star in the farthest reaches of space... For a second, his head was full of visions of butterflies exploding in swarms out of the long meadow grass and night skies full of stars.

"Do you feel that?" said the grey kitten, "It's like we were meant to be together. Oh, we're going to have such fun!" She laughed, and her laugh was like the tinkling of a tiny bell.

MISSION IMPUSSIBLE

In 2016, we celebrated the arrival into The Critter Room of John's fiftieth set of fosters and the occasion was marked by, among other things, the compilation of a scrapbook containing letters, poems, artwork and stories from fans from all over the world. My own contribution was this little tale, which unites all of the Kitten Cam mothers and at last rights a great wrong—the fact that I never wrote a story for Laika. "Mission Impussible" features a cameo appearance by the lovely Lady Peaches, who sadly crossed The Bridge at the end of 2016. She was a wondrous lady who will not be forgotten.

It was the Circle to beat all Circles. Suggestions had been suggested, suggestions had been rejected, feelings had—inevitably—been hurt, then soothed, then forgotten but, eventually, when they had managed to weed out the impossible, the improbable, the implausible, and the downright dangerous, they were left with a single plan which they all agreed was achievable. Probably.

Roles had been assigned, each according to their special talents. Rosemary was The Mastermind, as usual. There were other cats in the group just as smart as she, but the imposing calico had seniority—It Was Written, she always said (although, significantly, Rosie was the only one who could read, so nobody could dispute this). She would co-ordinate the plan and, more importantly, provide The Words.

Mimi, with her exceptional engineering skills, was nominated The Cracker. There was no entrance, exit, box, cupboard or treat bag that she couldn't unlock, prise apart or, if necessary, shoulder-charge. For the occasion, she decided to revert to her former name. "Codename: Laika!" she grinned, thoroughly enjoying the drama, while Rosie sighed and rolled her eyes.

Glados, a skilled gatherer and mover of small objects, was appointed The Scrounger, assigned to procure the tools and materials they would need. She was thrilled to learn that the list of requirements included a particular kind of wand toy and she knew exactly where one could be found. It had been carelessly stashed by a hoomin in a position where it just played havoc with the Feng Shui and needed to be removed post haste. That would be the easy bit, she thought, as she studied the remainder of the list. The other items would be challenging, to say the least, requiring at least two naps to cogitate and a bowl of crunchies to formulate a strategy. She curled up and closed her eyes, ready to tackle the task at hand.

Lacey had roused herself from her dad's lap for long enough to accept the responsibility of acquiring The Gift. It had been her idea, and she was proud of her own inventiveness. There had been a short, but heated, debate as to its suitability, but she had reminded them of his obvious love for the stuff. "He must have roomfuls of it by now..." she had said, and the others were obliged to concur. Despite having thoroughly embraced The Path to Inner Peace in her forever home, underneath, she was still the same fastidious Kari who had baffed her kittens until they shone and trimmed their whiskers down to the nubs. She could certainly be trusted to select a gift of the ideal shape and size, and to lovingly polish it until she could see her face in it. She had spent much of her relaxation time observing, through one open eye (sometimes the blue one, sometimes the gold one) her hoomin mama as she twisted and stitched her yarns into wonderful things which were NOT kitty beds, apparently, (such a waste) and she was pretty sure she was up to the task of fashioning a presentable gift bow. To that end, she had quietly liberated a length of bright wool from its basket and secreted it under a sofa cushion. With nothing to do now but prepare The Gift and await the signal, she closed her eyes and resumed her quest for the Inner Light.

Finally, Ripley and Alice, both dark in colour and therefore able to slip in and out of the shadows practically unseen were chosen as The Couriers, the cats who would carry the precious cargo to its destination. "Don't do the thing with the eyes," said Laika to Ripley. "They'll light up like a couple of searchlights if a car goes past." Ripley assured her that "the eyes" were a thing of the past. "You concentrate on your task—I'll concentrate on mine." She sniffed, and returned to her household chores—in this case, helping to keep her hoomins' daily newspaper nice and flat. She was in charge of the sports section.

The Circle broke up and they all returned to their normal lives. Well, most of them did. Laika, however, began a strict fitness regime. First, she went carb-free, which suited Norbert no end as it meant extra crunchies for him, then she began a punishing regimen of late-night zoomies and furniture climbing, with a bit of jumping in and out of boxes in a manner guaranteed to baffle her hoomin thrown in. She would need to be honed and toned come the big night.

Glados quietly purloined the inappropriately-placed wand toy and secreted it in a dark corner under the sofa where the hoomins rarely ventured. She could just reach the feathery end of it at full stretch. She also dragged an empty treat box out of the garbage and into the same location. Every night, she would haul it out and set to nibbling at the cardboard, taking care to be neat, until she had at last liberated a sizeable rectangle, brightly coloured on one side, but unmarked on the other. As for the last item on her list— a harness and leash—she had drawn a blank. In the quiet of the night, she conveyed this fact to Laika, who told her not to worry— she would think of something.

Kari lined up several possible candidates for The Gift, inspecting them thoroughly for shape, colour and texture, before selecting the one she felt came closest to perfection. She waited patiently until it was well matured before she began to roll it over the carpet. And roll it and roll it and roll it... until the surface was entirely free of lumps, bumps, crevices and craters. Then she rolled it some more, until it began to take on a soft sheen. When it was as smooth and as glossy as an egg, she carefully extracted her length of pink wool and, co-opting Tucker onto the team to help her keep the knot tight while she fiddled with the loose ends, she was able to fashion a passable looking bow. The loops were a bit uneven and the ends of the wool were damp and chewed, but she nonetheless glowed with pride as she stood back to admire the finished article. Tucking the gift away under the sofa cushion, she took up position on top of it to ensure that it remained undiscovered by her hoomins. It would have been a little tricky to explain. And she waited.

Rosie sat on her cat tree in the window and consulted her celestial calendar. She knew all the stars by name, knew where they should be in the night sky and at what time of year, knew all the planets by their size and brightness and, of course, knew all about the phases of the Moon. She watched its various waxings and wanings and, by mentally calculating the visible surface area plus its distance from the Great Cat's Eye, multiplying that by the number of meals she had eaten since Thursday, dividing the total by the reciprocal of paw and swatting Socks round the back of the head for good measure, she was able to ascertain the optimum date for their foray. She was very excited and she told George this. She told George everything. She almost forgot to tell the others, but remembered just in time and sent out the signal. As the sun disappeared below the horizon on the big night, she blew a kiss to George's star—just for luck—and headed off via the loose window that her people had yet to discover, leaving Socks to apply his dead weight to the slumbering hoomins. She had all The Words in her head, but she recited them under her breath anyway. The Words, if nothing else, had to be perfect.

Laika slipped out as quietly she was able. She too left her companion to keep their hoomin well pinned down, lest she should notice the absence of fifty per cent of the feline population of her home. Trying to dislodge a sleeping Norbert would be like trying to shift a tree. The hoomin was going nowhere. As she approached the corner of the street, she spotted Glados waiting for her, a paper carrier bag considerably larger than herself held between her teeth by its handles. "Fnarrrr pnut thwik arrff?" asked Glados. "Put the bag down, dear," said Laika. "Any trouble getting here?" asked Glados again. "No. What's in the bag?" She peered inside. There was the stick of a feather toy—feather removed with maximum prejudice—a small screwdriver, a ball of twine, the all-important rectangle of card and a pink stuffed mouse. "A mouse...?" Laika looked quizzically at Glados. "Habit." Glados replied with a shrug. At that moment, she bristled, her hackles rising, and her back arched. Behind Laika, two large black male cats had stepped out of the shadows and were approaching fast. "Whatever you do, don't turn round..." she hissed. Laika immediately turned round. "Hello boys!" she said to the approaching cats. "Glados, meet Boris and Pavel—my lads." "I'm Buzzy, mum," said the one called Pavel. "Yeah, whatever..." said his mother, barely listening. "My muscle," she explained. Pavel ducked under a nearby plant and hauled out a red leather harness and leash. "It's Valya's. She'll be livid if I don't bring it back." "Carry it for your mother, please," ordered Laika, "and Boris, be a gentleman and take Glados' bag."

The boys rolled their eyes at each other—nothing had changed. The bizarre quartet set off, their mission that night to liberate any cat who was unable to do so themselves, or to collect a signature from those who could not attend. And so it was that Lady Peaches was astonished, just a few minutes later, to awake from a pleasant snooze on the windowsill to find a sizeable torbie cat suspended outside her upstairs window, swinging gently from side to side. She had had fish for dinner that night, which often caused her to have vivid dreams, so she dismissed the sight as a hallucination. The hallucination waved cheerily to her as it slowly rotated on the end of a red cord. As she came round again to face Peaches, she signalled to the old cat to push open the window. She introduced herself. "You knew I was coming, didn't you?" she asked Peaches. "Did I, dear? I don't know... my memory isn't what it was. Would you like to pop in for a drink and some crunchies? They're tuna." "Not just now, thank you." The harness was beginning to chafe. "How are you doing that, dear? Some sort of anti-gravity device?" Various squeaks and grunts were audible from the region of the roof, and Peaches swivelled her head to look up to where Boris and Pavel, teeth gritted and ears flat with exertion, were hanging on to the red leash. "Oh, hello," she called. "Would you like to pop in for a drink and some crunchies? Tuna..."

"Seriously, Peaches honey, we can't stop. We just need you to sign this." She handed the piece of card to Peaches. "Oh, of course. Yes, I remember this. It's for that lovely man... what's his name? Don. That's right. Oohh, we had some lovely naps together, he and I. Do you know... I wouldn't be here now if it wasn't for him and his friends? I remember one evening..." "MAAAAAAM!" A wail from Boris and a jerking of the leash cut short the old cat's reminiscences. She nose-booped the card and whispered her message before handing it back to a now gradually descending Laika. Laika jerked a thumb upwards and, slowly, painfully and noisily, the boys began to reel her in. As she disappeared, Peaches called after her. "Sorry you couldn't stop.

Maybe next time, eh? We'll have some nice crunchies... they're tuna... and bring those lovely boys with you."

At their next stop, Miss Janine gave her profound apologies from atop a tottering pile of Amazon boxes. She would love to attend but her presence was required at a grand gift opening to celebrate the birthday of her sons. However, she would, of course, be honoured to sign the card. Laika pushed it under the door and Janine carefully rubbed her right cheek across it and quietly delivered her message, before passing it back. There was a muffled crash from inside the house. "Gotta go..." said Janine, "Oh, Egon...!"

They went from house to house, apartment to apartment, prising open windows, doors, air vents and letter boxes and, with each home visited, the little feline convoy grew longer and longer. They were all there—Miranda, Marie, Ripley, Kari, Hazel, Dory, Alice, Libby, Marge, Willow, Miss Honey, Nala Se, Smooch—all the Critter Room mothers, snaking their way in and out of the shadows, darting into doorways and behind hedges to avoid headlights and humans, Glados carrying the precious card and the feather stick (and the screwdriver, twine and pink stuffed mouse), and Laika checking the road ahead and managing to lead the way and chivvy up the convoy from the rear at the same time. She was in her element. Boris and Pavel (who was now allowed to revert to his given name of Buzzy) departed, kissing their mother goodbye and—yes, promising to behave, keep their rooms tidy and wash behind their ears, and the girls moved on to their important rendezvous.

When they finally arrived at the appointed place, Rosie was already there, tapping her claws on the ground impatiently. "Come on!" she scolded. "We don't want to lose the Moon." They looked around them—it wasn't exactly a sylvan glade, more a patch of waste ground with the cold remains of some sort of bonfire. This, as it turned out, was why the location had been selected. "I need something to write with," she explained, "and this black stuff where the wood has burned works well. Glados, bring me the wand toy." Glados complied. "Now," said Rosie, "I need you to help me guide it. I'm going to use the stick end to make my letters." Hazel and Nala Se positioned themselves at the formerly feathered end of the wand and held it steady while Rosemary rubbed the tip into the blackened wood. Then, with her tongue between her teeth and a look of fierce concentration on her face, she slowly began to move the stick. The other cats watched in wonder as marks began to appear on the card. The toy didn't make the best stylus, and Rosie's backup staff sometimes pulled when they should have pushed, but gradually the words emerged, a little smudged and somewhat wayward, but clear enough to get their message across. "Now..." said Rosie, sitting down to regain her equilibrium, "...we wait for the right moment".

They all sat, silent and motionless, watching the skies—apart from Marge, who was overcome by a sudden urge to vigorously baff her underparts, until a sharp "Ahem!" from Rosie brought her back to the job in hand. At last, the clouds parted and bathed the gathering in a pool of silver. If anyone had been passing right then, they would probably have hurried on by, unaware that, if they had stopped for a while to watch, they would have witnessed one of the rarest and most magical events in all of nature—a circle of she-cats invoking their deity, the Moon, and channelling Her power into one earthly object—a small scrap of cardboard.

One by one, each of the cats made their invisible mark on the card—a nose boop, a cheek rub, a lick of the tongue, more than just a signature—a tiny piece of their hearts. They knew of no better way to convey their love and gratitude than that. Then they moved in close, so their whiskers were touching, to form an unbroken ring of power. Rosemary, her paw held over the card, recited the prayer.

"Oh Lady Moon, weaver of dreams, bringer of light and giver of hope, hear our prayer this night for one special hoomin, whose goodness has changed our world for the better, and to whom we all owe at least one of our lives.

Grant him the Power of the Whisker, so that he may always find his way out of a tight spot. Grant him the Power of the Nose, so that he may always know his friends from his enemies. Grant him the Power of the Ear, so that he may always keep one step ahead of danger. Grant him the Power of the Eye, so that he may always see the light in the darkness. Grant him the Power of the Floof, so that he may always find warmth in a cold world. And grant him above all the Power of the Paw, the protection of all cat-kind—so that he may pass through this world with a light tread, without fear, harming nothing, his path taking him unburdened to wherever he needs to go.

May the light of the Moon fall upon him and all he holds dear."

They all spoke this last line in unison. At a nod from Rosemary, Smooch, his Jubilee mama, stepped forward and proudly applied the only visible mark to the card. The job was done.

Kari handed over The Gift to Alice while Ripley took the card between her teeth and the two of them set off together. Tempted though they were to stay and chat together until dawn, the others instead touched noses in farewell and stole away into the night, back to their own homes. Alice and Ripley, meanwhile, approached the house which held so many memories for them. Looking up, they saw a dark, worried little face with eyes like saucers staring down at them from the familiar upstairs window. "That could be me, all those moons ago." said Ripley, wistfully. "Me too," said Alice, "Lucky girl. She's just at the beginning of her journey." They deposited their precious cargo close to the front door and turned to leave, but first they looked back up at the window and gave a slow blink to the nervous young mother who was watching them. "If only she knew what was to come..." said Ripley and, as the first hint of dawn began to light the horizon, they crept silently away into the shadows.

Later that morning—much later—he opened his front door and was astounded to find, on his doorstep, a perfectly smooth cat turd, polished to a shine and tied with a pink woollen bow, and a damp, stained and dog-eared scrap of card in the centre of which there was a single, smudged paw print and, crudely scratched out in charcoal, the words,

"And thank you, girls," he said, and tucked the card into his pocket.

ADOPTION DAY

Adoption Day is always a combination of excitement, fear, sadness and joy. For Patience and her kittens, Tommy, Deuces and Diplomat, it was no different. For two small kittens on the other side of The Bridge, it was magical.

Klondike sat on a flat stone on the edge of the meadow, soaking up warmth from above and below. The sun was high and there was no shade nearby, but he was enjoying the sensation of being slowly and pleasantly cooked from the ears down. He imagined he could hear his fur quietly sizzling. The residual heat from the stone warmed his underside at the same time—he would be done to a turn, he mused, yawning. A honey bee hummed past followed closely by Ladybug, her tiny legs going full pelt to keep up. All morning, she had been galloping about the meadow, squealing and laughing in delight as she completely failed to catch butterflies, wasps, and damsel flies. Catching them wasn't really the point. The fun was in the chase. Klondike grinned as she whizzed past again, going in the other direction, having given up on the bee and now intent on bringing down a fat, noisy maybug. For a while, it looked as if Ladybug might actually catch up to her quarry, slow and clumsy as it was, so she stopped her pursuit and flopped down next to her brother, panting slightly from her exertions.

"Do you know?" she said, "If I'd been born in Britain, I'd be called Ladybird."

"Who told you that?" asked Klondike.

"Er... a British cat!" she declared. "Ladybugs are called ladybirds in Britain."

"But you're named after a card game," he reminded her.

"Oh... well, maybe card games are called different in Britain too."

"Maybe. Come on, we're going for a walk." Klondike hopped off his stone onto the cool grass and had a good, invigorating stretch—front paws together first, and then back paws one at a time.

"Where are we going?" asked Ladybug, eyeing a juicy looking moth as it skittered past.

"To The Bridge," said her brother. "Keep up, or you'll get lost." He strode off, out of the meadow and onto the little rough path that lead to the edge. Neither kitten had been back to The Bridge since they had arrived weeks earlier, tiny and lost, to be greeted by a crowd of cats and kittens who all seemed to be expecting them. The journey from being frightened and lonely to feeling safe and loved was exactly the same length as that taken from The Bridge to the party meadow. Ladybug had made it borne on the back of a huge, shaggy, cream coloured cat, as the welcome committee was afraid that her petite frame and extremely small legs would delay them reaching the sumptuous tea which awaited them. Klondike was proud that he had made the journey on his own feet, but then he was almost twice the size of his sister.

"Why are we going to The Bridge?" asked Ladybug, trotting briskly to keep up with her larger brother.

"Not sure," he replied. "I just think it's time we went. We'll be able to see them, if we dare to take a peek."

"See who?"

"Our family, of course."

Ladybug sat down on the path, wide-eyed. "Really? I think that might make me sad."

"Well, you don't have to look, but I think you should. I don't think it'll make you sad at all."

"Hmmm…"

They continued on their way, pausing to drink at the little brook, then hopping onto the big stones to cross it, then up the grassy bank which led to the birch glade with its velvety turf and dancing shadows. Bug cheered up when she felt the springy grass under her paws, and pounced and leaped after the fluttering leaves. Seeing her spinning and jumping, full of glee, Klondike was unable to resist the temptation to join in the game, allowing himself, just for a while, to drop his persona as the sensible, responsible one. He was a thoughtful kitten, with wisdom beyond his years and he was very protective of his little sister but, every now and then it did him good to just be a kitten. Eventually, when their leafy prey had all been duly despatched, they emerged from the glade onto the broad greensward which ran along the cliff edge. Right in front of them, they could see the ancient trees whose gnarled and leafless boughs had twisted together to form an archway and, beyond that, The Bridge itself, disappearing as always into swirling fog.

Above the chasm, the sky appeared dark, even though it was a bright afternoon where the kittens stood. In that midnight blue expanse they could see a million twinkling stars, one for every soul who had crossed The Bridge. They could see their own, like tiny ruby chips close together, red and silver sparks shooting back and forth between them. As usual, the ground close to The Bridge was crowded with cats, some awaiting the arrival of friends and loved-ones, some checking up on the homes and families they had left behind. Ladybug and Klondike approached the edge with caution. The ground dropped away vertically like a sheer cliff face and there was nothing below but darkness—it was a scary sight, even though the kittens knew they were safe.

"There!" Klondike pointed excitedly. After several minutes of peering into the void, Ladybug could finally see where he was pointing. "Look, there's Tommy and Deuces and Diplomat too. And the hoomin!"

"Where's mama?" asked Bug, craning her neck.

"There she is, behind the boys."

"What's happening?" The scene looked unfamiliar. There was light and noise and the room was full of people and bright objects and other cats. Klondike was unable to answer his sister.

"It's adoption day." The kittens turned to see an adult cat, whose face was familiar although they couldn't recall her name right now. "Keaira," she reminded them. "I come here often— usually I come to check up on two young friends of mine who went back over recently. But I also come for adoption days. They make me so happy."

"What does it mean?" asked Klondike.

"It's when a kitten or a cat gets to go home with a special hoomin. They live together and they take care of each other and have wonderful lives. Your mama and brothers are being adopted today. Each of them will go to a new home with a hoomin who really wants them, and they will get good food, warm beds, lots of toys and lots of love. It's just the best life. It's lovely here, but sometimes I miss my hoomin."

"Will we still be able to see mama and our brothers after dopshun?" asked Ladybug, her lip wobbling a little.

"Of course. You can watch them grow up and become big, handsome boys."

"I wish we were being dopted..." Ladybug's lip continued to wobble. "It sounds lovely."

For a long time, the pair watched, fascinated, as their family crouched patiently in their cage while the people milled around them, occasionally reaching in to pet them. Then, one by one, they were lifted out and each was handed to a hoomin to cuddle. Even though the kittens had little experience of people, they could see the joy and love written on their faces as they held their new babies for the first time.

"It must be wonderful to have hoomins love you so much..." Klondike mused.

"Yes it is," said Keaira. "Maybe one day... who knows?" She smiled at them, and then blew a kiss over the precipice to her own special person, before turning and walking back towards the birch glade.

The family was gone. Dopshun day was over, but the kittens continued to watch and wonder what it must be like to be loved so much by creatures so different from themselves. But then... something else was happening. Someone was speaking... and handing something to the big hoomin...

"Listen, Bug," said Klondike, "We've been adopted."

"What? Who? Who dopted us?"

"Lots of people. Even though they could never meet us and hold us and have us scratch their furniture and bite their toes... they still wanted us."

"Yay! We're dopted!" Ladybug hopped and bounced and chased her own tail in celebration. "Hoomins are wonderful!"

"Yes, they are aren't they?" Klondike gazed with awe as the little presentation concluded. He closed his eyes and he truly believed he could feel their love washing over him.

It was two satisfied kittens who made their way back that evening. Ladybug was full of excitement as usual, bursting to tell their friends that they were now dopted kittens with a huge hoomin family over on the other side. Klondike pondered. He wanted to say thank you somehow, but he wasn't sure how. Maybe it didn't matter—such caring hoomins would surely understand... He looked up to the now darkening sky and smiled. That would do.

So that night, when the Moon was at Her highest, if those special hoomins had cared to look upwards (as many like to do), they would have seen two stars, like tiny ruby chips, flashing red and silver fire towards them as two contented kittens curled up to sleep, happy in the knowledge that they were remembered with love.

THE ARRIVAL

Can a kitten change the world?

We're really glad you've come to stay
Just think of all the games we'll play.
And how much fun we'll have together,
I know we'll be best friends forever.
They've sent me here to take you back.
I've promised I will stay on track,
So we mustn't wander off or stray,
Or waste time playing on the way.

Ooh…!
Here—put your ear against this tree—
That humming sound's a bumblebee.
He really is a dapper fellow
In his velvet coat of black and yellow.
He'll let you chase him but, if caught
His temper runs a little short.
And so we let him stay ahead
And chase the dragonflies instead.
Then later, when the sun goes down
The moths come out, all plain and brown.
They dance beneath the stars all night
Their wings reflecting silver light
And with them dance the fireflies,
Like tiny golden kittens' eyes
Around our heads they glow and spark
A fiery ballet in the dark.

Ooh…!
Now look at how these dead leaves curl
You can take them to the stream and hurl
Them in the water, where they float—
A fleet of tiny kitten boats.
And if you bend your head and blow,
Away across the stream they go,
Until they reach some distant shore—
An unknown country to explore
And claim for all of Kittenkind
(And anyone we've left behind).

Now, this is how we cross the stream,
All roped together as a team,
Battered by the churning foam
Which tries to fling us off this stone
And drag us down into the depths...
No, really we just use these steps.
Across these little rocks we hop
And on the middle one we stop
To skim a stone and make a wish,
But careful not to scare the fish.

Ooh...!
And now we're on the other side
A great savannah, vast and wide
Where lions slink, hyenas lope
And cheetahs chase the antelope,
The zebras graze, the vultures soar
And we must cross—but not before
I've scaled the mighty look-out tree
To check it's safe—what can I see?

Ooh... er...!
A slightly angry Auntie Quark
Who said we must be home by dark
I think we might be slightly late
The other guests won't want to wait
For potted shrimp and seafood paste
And sardine sandwiches that taste
Like salty oceans on your tongue
And drip with oozy oils that run

Into your fur and make it sticky
(Which can make cleaning up quite tricky.)
Then, after games and cake and pie
We'll chant your praises to the sky,
And, once she's sure of who you are
The Lady Moon will light your star.
A tiny point of diamond light
To comfort mama every night.
We're nearly home—there's Cindy Lou
And Taps and Rain and Toothless too.
We're all your sisters, all your brothers,
Uncles, aunties, cousins, mothers...
All here to welcome you with love.
Me? I'm your favourite sister, Dove.

ONE PIECE AT A TIME

Can a kitten change the world? Can two kittens? Maybe they can, for one family at least...

The boy sat at the small table in the kitchen, ruminatively eating his cornflakes whilst reading the list of ingredients on the back of the packet. Making a mental note to Google "thiamine" and "niacin," to find out what they heck they actually were and whether their presence in his breakfast cereal was beneficial to his health and well being, he put down his spoon and reached for his tea mug. He liked to survey his domain over the rim of his red mug—the small, neat kitchen, his mother making his lunchtime sandwich and, in the corner of the room, two young cats tucking into their own breakfasts.

At least, one of them was tucking in. The fluffy tabby ate with gusto, her eyes closed in pleasure, a soft purr trying to make itself heard over the sound of her smacking lips. Her elegant companion looked sideways at her, one eyebrow raised, then continued with his mission to fastidiously remove every last scrap of sauce from the bowl without disturbing any of the meaty chunks.

"Honestly, Peter," said Honey, between mouthfuls, "I don't know how you became such a picky eater. The chunks are the best bit—the bit that gives you energy!"

"I'll come back to them later." said Peter. "I subscribe to the theory that grazing is a healthier dietary choice than just scarfing it down."

"They'll go all dry." said Honey, her tongue making a rasping noise as she licked clean the bottom of her plate.

"I like them like that," he lied.

The boy, having finished his breakfast, pushed back his chair and stood up. He took his school bag and coat off the peg on the wall, collected his packed lunch from the counter and headed for the front door. In accordance with what had become their daily routine, Honey sat on the windowsill washing the detritus of her meal off her

paws and face, while Peter trotted at the boy's heels to the front door, where the pair exchanged nose kisses before he left the house to run to the bus stop. A few minutes later, the ritual was repeated, but this time it was Honey who followed the mother to the door and kissed her goodbye as she left to go to work.

Peter and Honey had learned a lot in the months since they'd arrived at their forever home. They had learned that they couldn't both fit through the cat door at the same time, that the lady next door liked kittens, that the lady at the other next door didn't, that a sheep cannot be reasoned with, that the meadow behind the house reminded them of somewhere...

They had also learned that some things that are broken cannot be mended. The jar with the mayonnaise, for instance, and the wine glass which Honey knocked onto the kitchen tiles with one swish of her magnificent tail. Also, the green vase, the pile of empty plant pots, next door's hideous plaster gnome, the blue vase and the big sponge cake—although the creamy bits still tasted good even when licked off the door of the fridge. All of these infractions had been tolerated with good grace by their humans. Except for the picture. Honey hadn't meant to do it. She was just playing at "the floor is lava" with Peter and the picture—a framed photograph of a good-looking young man dressed in uniform—fell from the mantelpiece onto the hearth and the glass cracked. The mother shouted in anger and jumped up so suddenly that Honey took fright and ran out of the room to hide under the bed. Much later, the mother coaxed her out with a treat and picked her up and held her tight, burying her face into Honey's fur. Honey could feel a touch of damp on the back of her neck—not for the first time—and knew what she had to do.

For sometimes, the kittens had learned, human hearts could be broken too, and there was a hole in this home which, at times, threatened to suck all of the light and air and joy so far down into it that it could never return. They sincerely believed, however, that it was possible to mend a home and a human heart, one piece at a time. What's more, they believed that this was their mission, so they set about it with a will.

Whenever the mother was alone in the house, and she would put down her book, or her whisk, or her needle and retreat to her bedroom and curl up on her bed, Honey would make it her job to jump up beside her and to trill in her prettiest voice and roll onto her back and make air biscuits and to purr and to purr until, instead of weeping bitter tears into her pillow, the mother would run her hands over Honey's fur and lay her head next to the woolly belly and doze off listening to the safe comforting rumble, and the mother would remember a little what contentment felt like.

And whenever the boy sat alone in his room on a fine day, instead of joining his friends outdoors, Peter would make it his job to push his way in through the door and to pounce at the sunbeams and jump at the dust motes and to stalk imaginary prey and to chase his own tail until, instead of sitting and staring aimlessly into space, the boy would reach for the feather stick and the two of them would leap and spin and run and laugh, and the boy would remember a little what fun felt like.

One piece at a time.

* * * * *

It was early spring when the subject of birthdays came up.

"What do you want this year?" his mother asked.

There were plenty of things he needed, and a few things he wanted, but he knew money was tight and he had to keep his expectations low.

"I don't really know. I'll have to think about it." He really needed, and also wanted, new trainers, but the ones he'd set his heart on were hideously expensive and, let's be honest, better no trainers at all than the wrong ones. So, he didn't mention them and asked for time to consider instead.

"Maybe we can go out somewhere this year," she ventured.

"We don't have a car. It failed its MOT."

"Tom has a car..."

She knew even as she said it what his reaction would be. The boy's face reddened, he jumped to his feet and stomped off to his bedroom, slamming the door.

Peter instinctively followed, sensing that his services would be needed. Honey, likewise, moved to sit beside the mother's feet, ready to jump into her lap should things escalate. Finding the boy's door closed, Peter mewed quietly. It opened a crack, and he quickly snaked through the gap before it was slammed shut again.

The boy lay on his back on the bed, with Peter sitting on his chest, paws tucked in, in a tidy loaf position. He kept his steady, cornflower blue gaze on the boy's face as he ranted, through gritted teeth.

"I don't want him at my birthday... he's always here... hanging around mum... crashing about the place... him and that lolloping dog... you don't like the dog either."

Peter inclined his head. Actually, the dog was pretty civilised, considering. She'd always been polite to him and Honey, anyway. However, her body language was unpredictable, so both cats tended to keep out of her way.

"... and his stupid red sports car and his stupid green Land Rover and his filthy gumboots and his beard and his stupid posh voice..."

He tailed off temporarily devoid of any more things to hate about "The Man." The Man had begun to show up about a month previously. Firstly, he had called in with a trailer load of firewood for their wood burning stove, then he had called in with packets of chops and sausages for their freezer and mum had invited him to stay for coffee, then he had called in with some bottles of his home-made elderflower cordial and mum had made him lunch, then after that he had just begun to call in. The boy would sometimes come home from school and there would be The Man, sitting at the kitchen table like he belonged, with that lolloping dog lying on the floor and the kittens nowhere to be seen.

"If he thinks he can replace dad, he's got another think coming!" The boy spat out the words, teeth still gritted, face still red. "He's not my dad... what does he even do?" He pushed his balled up fists into his eye sockets, in a vain attempt to stop the tears from flowing.

"My dad was a soldier..." he told Peter, who already knew this. "He was always away, but it didn't matter 'cos he always came home, and then it was brilliant. He'd bring loads of presents and we'd have a big welcome home party and after that we'd go for bike rides and play football and go to the beach and play chess and we'd talk and talk... and then... he didn't come home." The boy opened his eyes to find himself gazing into the blue depths of Peter's. "I named you after him, Peter. I don't want a new dad... if I can't have the old one, I'd rather have no dad at all."

Peter extended his claws in a gesture intended to offer comfort. "Ow! That hurts!" The boy brushed Peter onto the floor and turned on his side, facing the wall. Peter, finding the bedroom door shut, exited via the open window.

"He hates him!" said Peter, later that evening. "We have to get rid of him!"

"No," said Honey. "She likes him and he helps her. We can't just get rid of him."

"But you always run under the bed when he arrives."

"So do you..."

"Hmmm... more research needed." The kittens agreed.

* * * * *

The Man came again the following day. He arrived in the late afternoon in the stupid red sports car, carrying a large box of tools, which he used to make various unpleasantly loud and unwarranted noises by hitting and scraping them against parts of the mother's car. To get a better view, Honey screwed up her courage and jumped onto the bonnet of the stupid sports car—which was toasty warm and very comfortable. She was unable to resist the urge to lie down and gently grill first one side, then the other, all the while keeping one eye (if that) on The Man and his activities.

"There you go, cat." She awoke from her doze to find him speaking directly to her. "New brake shoes and some filler for the hole in the exhaust—what do you think?" His hand came towards her and her ears flattened automatically. She couldn't help it—that fur on his face startled her every time. His hand kept on coming, and it tickled her behind the ears. She was surprised at his gentleness. She noted it down.

The man came again the following day, this time in the stupid green Land Rover. From out of the back, he extracted a large orange machine which began to roar and clank and judder, sending Honey flying through the cat door to the safety of the kitchen. Peter was feeling brave that day, but he retreated underneath a dense shrub, from which vantage point he could observe in relative safety. Up and down, up and down the man marched, pushing the noisy machine before him. Once, he paused, bent down and waggled his finger in the grass just in front of the machine's fearsome blades. A tiny mouse shot across the lawn and disappeared into a flower bed. Then, he continued until he had pushed the machine over every inch of the grass. "There you go, cat." His face appeared, upside down, in front of Peter. "Could be Versailles, eh?" He reached in and tickled Peter under the chin in a friendly fashion. Peter made a note.

By the end of a week, Peter and Honey had plenty of notes to compare.

"He fixed the car," said Honey.

"He saved the mousie," said Peter.

"He dug in the flower bed to make it easy for the robin to find insects,"

"He cut a hole in the fence so the hedgehogs can get through,"

"He made a little house out of wood just for the bees,"

"He planted catnip in pots, just for us,"

"He did? Where?" demanded Honey.

"So, what's our conclusion?" asked Peter

Both of them agreed that The Man was probably not so bad and at least deserved a chance. They would spring into action immediately. After dinner... and a nap.

*   *   *   *   *

The weekend of the boy's birthday dawned bright and clear. Spring was very much in the air and both he and his mother sat in the garden—she on the bench at the bottom end, he on an upturned bucket outside the kitchen door. It had been a difficult week. There had been arguments, prolonged silences, slammed doors and tears on both sides. The kittens had been busy, offering comfort to both their humans and, occasionally, taking refuge under the bed when the arguing threatened to get out of hand, but still no agreement had been reached. The boy didn't want The Man spoiling his birthday. The mother insisted that The Man was coming anyway. The kittens had formulated their strategy, which was simple.

"You take the dog; I'll take The Man..." Peter had said. Honey had grimaced a little, but accepted that this was the way it had to be.

The Man duly arrived, driving the stupid green Land Rover, and strode into the garden. The boy kept his head down, refusing to meet his eyes. The lolloping dog—actually a mostly-white Staffie with bright button eyes and a cheery demeanour, followed at his heels and rolled comically onto her back on the grass as he sat down next to the mother. Peter watched as Honey approached the dog. He saw her plant her nose on the dog's exposed pink belly, causing the dog to roll onto her front, startled. The two animals were nose to nose... Peter hoped for the best. Meanwhile, he approached his young human, rubbed himself round his ankles, and then jumped up onto his lap as he sat morosely on his bucket. In the way that only Peter could, he gazed into the boy's eyes. Deep into them. A thought entered unbidden into the boy's head and, despite his determination to ignore The Man at all costs, he felt compelled to look across the garden to where Honey was happily licking the white dog's ear, while the mother and The Man giggled at the sight.

Peter hopped off the boy's lap and walked down the garden. The mother reached down to caress his ears as she often did but, to her surprise, Peter walked straight past her and sprang instead onto the lap of The Man. The boy watched, taken aback and somewhat jealous, as his cat blatantly nose-kissed and scent marked this most unwelcome of visitors. Peter turned in his direction again and a new thought popped uninvited into the boy's head. He got up from his bucket and found himself walking down the garden, towards the bench, the dog, Honey, Peter, his mother and The Man.

"Hi. Happy birthday," said The Man.

"Thanks," said the boy. He sat down on the bench alongside his mother and Peter immediately moved in to make himself comfortable on his lap. Briefly, boy and cat locked eyes once more. For some reason, the boy felt a little less hostile towards The Man—he wasn't sure why.

"I've got some errands to run," said The Man. "Would you like to come with me?"

"Why?" asked the boy.

"I think you'll enjoy them."

His mother smiled and nodded. "Er... OK." He was rather dubious about this.

He climbed reluctantly into the passenger seat of the stupid green Land Rover. The lolloping dog, whose name he learned was Sally, jumped into her compartment behind the seats and they drove off.

"I remember this place!" the boy said, as they arrived at the gate of a forested area a few miles outside the village. "We came on a nature walk when I was at junior school." He didn't remember much about it, except that it had been cold, his feet had got wet, but it had been fun to escape the classroom for a couple of hours.

"It's a nature reserve," said The Man. "I'm the warden here—that's my job."

"Wow!" said the boy. "I thought you were a builder or something."

"Never assume..." The Man laughed. "Come on—I'll introduce you to some of my neighbours."

For the next two hours, boy and man walked around the woods, Sally at their heels, stopping at a rickety looking barn to check on the barn owl who was nesting in a special box near the roof, then peering underneath it with a flashlight to spot the vixen who lay under there, calm but watchful, awaiting the birth of her cubs, then inside the hollow tree, where the light revealed a cluster of what appeared to be small leather drawstring purses stuck to the wood by their strings.

"Horseshoe bats," The Man explained. "They're a secret—you must promise never to tell anybody they are there."

"Why not?"

"They're a protected species. You need a special licence even to view them, let alone handle them. I have to count them regularly to check that the colony is thriving."

"Wow! What a great job." said the boy, genuinely impressed.

They carried on with their walk, taking in the badger sett (no badgers to be seen at this time of day) the wooden nesting boxes nailed high up in the trees, a magnificent stag beetle hidden under some damp leaves and plenty of squirrels scuttling about on the forest floor. "Trying to remember where they hid their nuts..." said The Man, laughing.

The boy returned home much happier than when he left. His mother and the cats were still in the garden, but now there was also a big cake and a parcel wrapped in fancy paper on the garden table. The cake turned out to be chocolate, while the parcel contained the longed-for trainers.

"It's OK," whispered his mother. "I just moved a few things around... we can manage. How was the nature reserve?"

"Brilliant!" he said. "I'd love to go again sometime and see if the barn owl has her chicks and the fox has her cubs and..."

"I hope you will come again," said The Man. "And, to make it a little easier for you..." He disappeared round the side of the house and returned, wheeling a sturdy-looking bicycle. "Look, it's not new, but I've fixed it up and put heavy duty tyres on it and decent gears. It should make a good off-roader."

The boy was genuinely lost for words. He had long since outgrown his old bike, and there hadn't been enough money for a new one. His dad had promised to buy him one, of course, but...

Peter hopped up onto the boy's lap and they touched noses, causing a sharp snap of static.

132

"Look," said The Man, quietly. "I'm not trying to replace your dad. I can never do that. But, well, grownups get lonely sometimes and me and your mum—we're both on our own, so we're just keeping each other company. And you and me... I reckon we could be good mates. That's all. Think about it."

The boy's vision misted up and he gave a small sniffle. "Thanks for the bike, Tom."

"You're very welcome, David."

* * * * *

The sky was changing from pink to purple as the kittens sat on a small mound of soft grass in the meadow behind the house. They loved to sit here at dusk whenever they could, watching the stars appear one by one in the darkening sky.

"They say that the stars are the eyes of our ancestors." said Honey, not for the first time.

"Not just our ancestors," added Peter, "But of all the cats and kittens who have crossed over The Bridge."

They were waiting for their favourite stars to appear.

"Do you think we did good today?" asked Peter.

"Yes, pretty good," replied Honey. "It wasn't all us, of course, The Man and his lolloping dog helped."

"Sally. Her name is Sally."

The kittens fell silent as familiar stars began to peep through the velvety blueness. They watched for these every night because, fanciful though it probably was, they had the feeling that, somehow, these stars were watching them back. There was the small one that shone with an emerald light and, close by, its larger companion, amber like the flare of a match (the kittens believed that these two were close friends, never to be separated), the tiny twin stars like fiery ruby chips, the glittering diamonds that seemed to dance around each other, full of joy, the cluster of soft pearls that seemed to be the centre of things (wise lady cats, Honey thought)...

"Look," said Honey, "there's one more lady cat tonight," and, sure enough, a new star glowed with an inner fire, like an opal. "I wonder who she was..."

The lights were on in the house and the lure of a meal and a comfy spot on the sofa was strong. The muffled sound of laughter drifted through the dusk as the kittens pushed through the gap in the fence and trotted across the garden to their cat door. Far away, just for a moment, the stars seemed to burn a little brighter.

* * * * *

"There you are," said Tuffy, as they leaned over the edge. "Yes, it's true that we can leave broken hearts behind us when we leave, but it's also true that we can help to mend them while we are there. That family still has a long journey ahead of them, but they will have good companions along the road."

"One piece at a time..." said Peaches, and the two old cats turned their backs on the bridge and walked together through the twilight to the meadow.

ABOUT THE AUTHOR

Jill Pickford was born in London, but her family left the city for the 'burbs when she was a child. After various schools so unremarkable they could no longer be bothered to exist, she attended Birmingham University to train as a teacher. She chose not to follow a career as an educator when she realised that most school children were bigger than she was, knew everything already, and tended to hunt in packs. Instead, she used her university years to enjoy copious quantities of real ale and hitchhike around Britain and Europe in pursuit of rock and roll. After graduation, a succession of office jobs followed, including a stint working for a national TV broadcaster, an enjoyable interlude brought to an untimely halt by one Margaret Thatcher. She currently works part time as a shipping manager for a small importing company run by maniacs.

Jill is happily single and lives with her rescue cat, Sybil, in a 17th Century cottage with dodgy electrics, a lousy internet connection and three sheds. In her spare time, she enjoys quilting and patchwork, playing two chords on the ukulele (she's currently learning a third), and attempting to write a full length novel about pirates for junior humans.

Despite being English, Jill doesn't drink tea, thinks the jam should go on the scone before the cream, and hangs her toilet roll with the loose end at the back, just to annoy visitors.

SING TO THE MOON

COME AND CHAT.

Please visit our Facebook Group, "Sing to the Moon" at
www.facebook.com/groups/Singtothemoon
Download a free glossary of terms to enhance
your reading pleasure.
Order copies at www.singtothemoonbook.com.
All royalties benefit Purrfect Pals.

Email the author at
Singtothemoon@groups.facebook.com